PRAISE FOR *QUALITATIVE LITERACY*

"Instead of judging qualitative research by the standards of other methods, Mario Luis Small and Jessica McCrory Calarco consider the purpose and aspirations of in-depth interviewing and ethnography and then offer criteria with which to evaluate if a piece of research hits the mark (or not). At once practical and sophisticated, *Qualitative Literacy* reflects the wisdom of two of the most talented qualitative researchers in the field today. It is an invaluable resource for methods teachers, funders, policy makers, and students."

MARY PATTILLO, author of *Black Picket Fences: Privilege and Peril among the Black Middle Class*

"This excellent, accessible book is written by authors with an impeccable reputation in the field. It brings focus to what we know and agree on as practitioners of qualitative research and how we should be thinking about the craft versus how it is typically taught."

D'LANE R. COMPTON, Full Professor of Sociology, University of New Orleans

"This is a stellar book. The authors have crafted a clearly written manuscript that will be useful both for teaching and as a handbook for practitioners. I have not seen anything quite like it, and this book helps me think reflexively about my own work and that of my students."

TANYA GOLASH-BOZA, Professor of Sociology, University of California, Merced

THE ATKINSON FAMILY
IMPRINT IN HIGHER EDUCATION

The Atkinson Family Foundation has endowed this imprint to

illuminate the role of higher education in contemporary society.

The publisher and the University of California Press Foundation gratefully acknowledge the generous support of the Atkinson Family Foundation Imprint in Higher Education.

Qualitative Literacy

Qualitative Literacy

A GUIDE TO EVALUATING
ETHNOGRAPHIC AND
INTERVIEW RESEARCH

Mario Luis Small
Jessica McCrory Calarco

UNIVERSITY OF CALIFORNIA PRESS

University of California Press
Oakland, California

© 2022 by Mario Small and Jessica Calarco

Library of Congress Cataloging-in-Publication Data

Names: Small, Mario Luis, 1974– author. | Calarco, Jessica McCrory, 1983–
    author.
Title: Qualitative literacy : a guide to evaluating ethnographic and interview
    research / Mario Luis Small, Jessica McCrory Calarco.
Description: Oakland, California : University of California Press, 2022. |
    Includes bibliographical references and index.
Identifiers: LCCN 2022005233 (print) | LCCN 2022005234 (ebook) |
    ISBN 9780520390652 (cloth) | ISBN 9780520390669 (paperback) |
    ISBN 9780520390676 (epub)
Subjects: LCSH: Ethnology—Qualitative research—Methodology. |
    Interviewing—Methodology.
Classification: LCC GN346 .S58 2022 (print) | LCC GN346 (ebook) |
    DDC 305.80072/1—dc23/eng/20220304
LC record available at https://lccn.loc.gov/2022005233
LC ebook record available at https://lccn.loc.gov/2022005234

31 30 29 28 27 26 25 24 23 22
10 9 8 7 6 5 4 3 2 1

For ARABELLA, LAYLA, LEO, and ODIN

Contents

Preface

This book is animated by a simple question. Suppose you were given two books, each based entirely on one year of ethnographic observation, and were told that one of them is a sound piece of empirical social science and the other, though interesting and beautifully written, is empirically unsound. What criteria would you use to tell the difference? One can ask the same question of a different kind of qualitative research. Suppose the two books were instead based on in-depth interviews with the same set of respondents, and you were informed that one is empirically sound and the other is not. What criteria would you use?

This question should matter to readers of the many qualitative studies regularly published on socially important topics: inequality, education, poverty and wealth, immigration, the family, crime and punishment, management and formal organization, public health, neighborhoods, labor, discrimination, housing and homeownership, aging, and the relationship between environment and society. Over the past two decades, qualitative research on each of these topics has come to be consumed by a large and diverse readership, a group that includes not only ethnographers and interviewers but also quantitative sociologists, demographers, economists, psychologists, applied statisticians, and others who themselves work on the topics, as well as the policy makers and legislators, think tank authors and foundation officers, practitioners and activists, journalists and lay readers who may not conduct formal research but whose work or beliefs are nonetheless deeply affected by what the field researchers report. All of these readers have a stake, in varying degrees, in the empirical soundness of the studies.

We have posed our criteria question to many people who would especially want to have an answer: quantitative social scientists who review qualitative studies in their topic of expertise for panels or journals; ethnographers of all stripes who produce such work themselves; private and national foundations' program officers who determine whether to fund such work; university deans, provosts, and presidents who evaluate such work for hiring and promotion; journalists who report on such work; and practitioners and policy makers who use such work in hopes of improving others' lives. When asked, some of these people proposed that experience and intuition should enable them to distinguish the empirically weak from the strong book—while also often admitting that they could not quite articulate what they would look for. Others pointed to criteria common in quantitative social science, such as reliability or representativeness, without offering a clear idea of how these would be applied to single-case ethnographies. Indeed, just about everyone who answered our question expressed some uncertainty, and the single most common answer was some version of the phrase, "I'm not sure."

That uncertainty partly reflects what one of us has called an absence of "qualitative literacy," the ability to read, interpret, assess, and evaluate qualitative evidence competently.[1] For several decades now, scientists, educators, and others have recognized the importance of *quantitative* literacy across society and have pushed for its dissemination with at least some success. School districts and colleges have buffered instruction to improve numeracy. Graduate training programs across the social sciences have deemphasized high theory in favor of empirical training in quantitative methods. In fact, the public discourse on the important topics we listed above is far more quantitatively literate than it was twenty or thirty years ago; newspapers and magazines routinely produce more and more accurately reported quantitative data and at times even make available the full dataset informing a story.[2]

Nevertheless, there has been no parallel increase in the public discourse's qualitative literacy. And this lapse is equally prominent in the social sciences themselves. For example, while most strong sociology PhD programs require training in quantitative research, the majority do not require courses in qualitative methods, even though their graduates produce many of the major ethnographies and interview studies on contemporary social problems.[3] Furthermore, even surface-level exposure to any qualitative coursework remains all but nonexistent in many of the other social sciences, such as psychology, political science, and economics—which would seem like the natural state of affairs but for the fact that today many of their graduates will have to evaluate qualitative research, within their topics of expertise, for foundations, tenure committees, and other venues. An economist teaching in an education graduate program, having never studied the evaluation of qualitative research, can nonetheless expect over the course of their career to vote on whether a school ethnographer deserves tenure. Indeed, in spite of the welcome intellectual openness of today's research on social problems, many quantitative researchers, and others in gatekeeping roles, are admittedly at a loss to explain how to evaluate qualitative empirical research, not on whether it is interesting or informative or well-written or a source of good ideas or of telling anecdotes, but on whether it is good social science.

That state of affairs represents a problem. The distinct kinds of knowledge produced by interview-based and participant observation research are indispensable to how much we know and how effectively we address inequality, housing, public health, discrimination, immigration, education, and the many other issues noted earlier. It is important to know whether a given set of qualitative findings is scientifically believable. And there is an enormous gap, we believe, between the knowledge needed to make that determination and the knowledge collectively possessed by those poised to assess, fund, support, report on, learn from, or make decisions on the basis of qualitative research. Our short book aims to fill that gap.

Introduction

In the not-too-distant past, qualitative and quantitative researchers in sociology and other disciplines were embroiled in a protracted conflict sometimes referred to as "the paradigm wars."[1] Field-workers accused their presumed opponents of conducting "positivistic," unreflective, or simple-minded research; quantitative analysts chided theirs for doing "soft" or unrigorous work, or of writing "just-so" stories with little scientific backing. To the extent it was a war, quantitative research clearly held the upper hand, as economics, demography, statistical analyses, and public opinion surveys deeply shaped national policy decisions.[2] But quantitative researchers who ignored fieldwork did so at their peril, as a vast body of ethnographic and interview-based research had documented and offered important insight into the experiences of many of the populations that those national discussions were concerned with, such as school students, the unemployed, married couples, low-income families, employers, and immigrants.[3] In all, the "wars" were a highly counterproductive conflict that made evident just how young, in historical terms, most social sciences are.[4]

But much has changed. While quantitative research arguably remains dominant in social science debates on important social problems, over the past two decades qualitative scholarship has dramatically shaped how scientists, policy makers, and the public think about inequality, poverty, race and ethnicity, gender, education, health, organizations, immigration, neighborhoods, and families.[5] It has helped us understand

why neighborhoods matter;[6]

how schools shape children's opportunities, expectations, and
    understanding of themselves;[7]

why people risk life and limb to cross the southern U.S. border;[8]

how employers evaluate potential hires;[9]

how people make decisions about marriage, employment, and
    child-rearing;[10]

how people manage legal institutions;[11]

how social and economic conditions affect people's everyday
    lives; and much more.[12]

In contrast to the past, economists, demographers, political scientists, and quantitative sociologists of all stripes today often cite qualitative studies in their own work and use those studies to generate hypotheses, illustrate discoveries, or interpret findings.[13] In turn, qualitative researchers have testified before Congress, helped governments set policy, advised local practitioners, contributed to the public discourse, and shaped how corporate and nonprofit boards invest and spend their resources.[14] At this juncture, the importance of interview and ethnographic methods to social science, and to society, is not in question.

But in spite of this progress, social scientists have not come to agree on what constitutes good qualitative social science—in fact, they do not even agree on whether qualitative research should be thought of as scientific, as opposed to merely informative, work.[15]

How to Assess Quality

Consider the recent history. In 1994, Gary King, Robert Keohane, and Sydney Verba's *Designing Social Inquiry* was supposed to lay to rest questions about the scientific foundations of qualitative studies by presenting clear guidelines for conducting and evaluating such work based on basic principles that guide quantitative research, such as reliability, unbiasedness, and efficiency.[16] The book was unusually detailed, comprehensive, and full of examples, promising to unite qualitative and quantitative researchers under a common view of rigorous empirical science. Instead, it sparked even more controversy.[17] To this day, the work strongly divides researchers, and qualitative researchers have repeatedly complained that its guidelines are inappropriate.[18]

In the early 2000s, the National Science Foundation (NSF), which funds social science scholarship, was facing an "increasing number of [submissions for] qualitative research projects" in sociology and recognized both that many reviewers did not know how to evaluate the work and that those who did seemed to disagree on the appropriate criteria.[19] The NSF convened a team of sociologists and later another of social scientists across several disciplines to clarify the standards by which qualitative research should be deemed rigorous and the criteria against which reviewers should evaluate proposals.[20] Distinguished social scientists participated in both teams, and each working group produced a volume of papers with summary guidelines.

But the researchers had so little in common in approach and perspective that many of their summary recommendations merely restated basic principles one would expect any proposal would have, rather than offering many new criteria specific to qualitative work. For example, the set of standards released by the first team recommended that researchers should "write clearly and engagingly for a broad audience," "locate the research in the relevant literature," "provide evidence of the project's feasibility," and so forth.[21] The second team had similar ideas, such as "situate the research in appropriate literature," "pay attention to alternative explanations," and "specify the limitations of the research and anticipate potential reviewer objections."[22] All of these recommendations have value, but they are suggestions that most experienced researchers in any discipline would already know to follow, rather than guidelines either specifically relevant or new to field-workers.

Not all of the NSF recommendations had this character; some were in fact distinctively appropriate to qualitative research. For example, the volumes recommended that researchers "assess the possible impact of the researcher's presence [and] biography"; discuss the researcher's "cultural fluency, language skill, . . . knowledge of particular research context"; and "describe and explain case selection."[23] But the guidelines nonetheless sparked controversy: at least one team member, who is one of the most distinguished and influential ethnographers in American history, openly challenged the NSFs conceptions of good research and produced an extraordinary minority report.[24] In the end, the NSF efforts, important though they were, did not bring closure to the questions the experts had been tasked to address.

In fact, over the ensuing years this ongoing ambiguity has contributed to several high-profile disputes involving fieldwork.

Famous ethnographers with widely discussed books have been accused of handling data poorly, of making implausible claims, and of rendering their findings unverifiable.[25] A recent book has "interrogated ethnography," proposing that claims in several major ethnographic studies do not stand up to legal standards of verification.[26] Indeed, some of the most contentious reviews of qualitative research today are produced by other qualitative researchers. Among the long list of controversies are those over grounded theory, "cowboy ethnography," replicability in recent ethnographies, exaggeration in anthropology, sampling in case studies, the value of interviews in studying behavior, and the ethics of masking identities in qualitative research.[27]

These controversies have left budding field-workers uncertain about how to conduct their own work; reviewers unclear about what signs of quality to look for; and scholars, journalists, and other consumers unsure about how to judge the work that qualitative researchers are generating.

Improving Social Science

That general uncertainty exists in a societal context where social science as a whole is looking more closely at its methods. In recent years, quantitative social science has experienced a reckoning, as common research practices in psychology, economics, political science, and quantitative sociology have come under extensive scrutiny. Critics have pointed to flaws large and small. Some problems are serious but relatively benign, faults of omission rather than commission; for example, studies in many subfields have been shown to be all too dependent on "WEIRD" samples, from white, educated, industrialized, rich, democratic respondents, a dependency that calls into question the work's empirical generalizability.[28] Other problems lie at the heart of scientific practice itself. Authors of high-profile quantitative studies have been found guilty of p-hacking (mishandling data to produce significant findings), HARKing (writing up hypotheses after the results are known), and even fabricating results.[29] In fact, the findings of numerous major experimental studies have been uncovered to be nonreplicable.[30] These practices undermine not only the quality of the science but also the public's trust, a problem that, in an era in which some politicians have sought to question the reliability of science, can be especially pernicious.[31]

Faced with this reckoning, however, quantitative researchers have instituted solutions. Journals have formalized many practices to improve how transparent and accountable quantitative studies are, including publishing more papers that aim to replicate prior findings, encouraging researchers to preregister their hypotheses in public repositories, requiring authors to publicly post the data and code that produced their analyses, and more.[32] At least some of these efforts are working. Malfeasance, mistakes, and questionable analytical decisions are often discovered quickly, discussed openly, and retracted as needed.[33] Bad research habits that were commonplace a decade ago are increasingly rare in the disciplines' best journals, as editors impose greater transparency, expect multiple robustness checks, and require making code and data easily available to reviewers.

These developments might have been great news for qualitative researchers but for the fact that many of the recommended practices are inappropriate for their work. For example, calling for researchers to replicate more ethnographies will often make no sense: an observational case study of a single event—for example, the Arab Spring or the George Floyd protests—cannot be replicated, since a future researcher cannot return to the past, recreate the event, and experience what the real-time observer did.[34] Similarly, requiring all field-workers to preregister their hypotheses would undermine major traditions in which the research is inductive; an ethnographer who is entering a study site without intending to test a prior hypothesis would have nothing to preregister.

In recent years, some qualitative researchers have proposed alternative ways of increasing the transparency of qualitative research.[35] Some scholars have discouraged ethnographers from anonymizing a field site unless necessary.[36] Others have called for interviewers to make de-identified transcripts publicly available.[37] But these proposals are not themselves universally agreed upon.[38] Moreover, they will be inappropriate for many kinds of projects, such as those in which identification poses too great a risk to participants or in which complete de-identification would render a set of transcripts all but meaningless. Finally, while increasing transparency will improve some kinds of work, it cannot be the heart of the solution to our problem, for it does not inherently distinguish good from bad work. Consider the proposal to resist anonymizing field sites: many weak ethnographies are open about where they were conducted, while in contrast, one of the most important ethnographies in history, William Foote Whyte's *Street Corner Society*, anonymized its site by calling it "Cornerville."[39]

While transparency might improve accountability, it still does not address our motivating question: how to assess the soundness of qualitative work. We have posed this question—what criteria would you use to distinguish empirically sound from unsound qualitative social science?—to many researchers across methodological perspectives and disciplines, including not only sociologists but also economists, psychologists, and statisticians, and across career stages, from senior scholars to graduate students beginning their fieldwork. Many have confessed that they ultimately do not know how they would answer. Our objective is to present a nonexclusive set of criteria applicable to any social scientist conducting in-depth interviews or participant observation. Our criteria will likely be recognizable by any qualitative researcher who conducts field-based research, since, as we shall see later, and despite their public epistemological debates, field-workers often demonstrate tacit agreement about quality in craftsmanship. We begin by clarifying some terms.

What Is "Qualitative Research"?

In a strict sense, there is no such thing as "qualitative research."[40] There is no single research practice, perspective, attitude about data, or approach to social science that all scholars who have used that term to describe their work follow. As one of us has written,

> Some use the term "qualitative" to describe all small-sample studies, regardless of whether the analysis is formal, because they consider those studies to lack statistical generalizability. Others use "qualitative" to characterize any approach in which units (such as organizations or nations), regardless of their number, are analyzed as cases rather than divided into variables, such as studies of revolutions in which countries are assessed in light of their particular historical circumstances. Still others use the term to refer only to studies that rely on hermeneutic or interpretive, rather than positivistic orientations. Because of these differences, the quantitative versus qualitative opposition has been used to contrast many kinds of alternative studies: large-n versus small-n, nomothetic versus idiographic, causal versus interpretive, variable-based versus

case-based, explanatory versus descriptive, probabilistic versus deterministic, and numerous others.[41]

One way of making sense of this heterogeneity is to understand that "qualitative" can refer to at least one of three different elements of the research project: the *type of data*, the method of *data collection*, or the approach to *data analysis*: "The first refers to that which has been collected for study; examples are interview transcripts, . . . newspaper clippings, field notes, and administrative records. The second refers to the means for obtaining data," such as interviewing or participant observation.[42] "The third refers to the means for making sense of the collected data."[43] To analyze the data, a researcher can choose among a broad range of both specific techniques, such as open versus closed coding of interview transcripts, and general approaches, such as grounded theorizing versus the extended case method.[44]

No type of data or method of data collection requires any specific analysis technique. One can use interview transcripts to write extended biographical narratives or to run statistical regressions.[45] One can use observational field notes to write classic ethnographies or to produce formal quantitative analyses.[46] Thus, there is little sense in trying to propose a single definition of "qualitative research." Our book uses the term merely as shorthand.

Our Focus

Methods of Data Collection

Still, our focus is narrow. Among the three elements—types of data, method of data collection, and type of analysis—our main focus is on methods of data collection, which require us to discuss also the quality of the data. We discuss how to assess, based on the finished text, whether the interviews or ethnographic field notes were collected effectively (and thus produced good data).[47] Two questions follow: Why focus on the methods of collection? Why lump in-depth interviewing and participant observation?

WHY WE FOCUS ON METHODS OF DATA COLLECTION. The primary reason we focus on data and methods, not on analytical approaches, is scope. The many schools of thought in qualitative research, including grounded theorists, ethnomethodologists, extended case researchers, feminist epistemologists, critical race ethnographers, survey-informed interviewers, statistics-driven inferential analysts, and many more, differ dramatically among themselves in what they view as the purpose of qualitative research, in how they frame research questions, and in what elements of the social world they believe are worth observing, all of which inevitably affects how they analyze data.[48] The points of divergence are too numerous for us to fully examine here. Imagine, for comparison, a book on how to evaluate survey research that not only attempted to discuss data collection methods (sample selection, power analysis, stratification and clustering, questionnaire design, etc.) but also tried to incorporate approaches to analyzing the data (frequentist and Bayesian perspectives, least squares and maximum likelihood estimation, continuous and categorical outcome models, fixed- and random-effects models, instrumental variables, matching and propensity score models, etc.). The task would require several volumes. Similarly, discussing how to detect the quality of the data collected, and of the method for doing so, on the basis of the finished book or article is sufficiently complex. Adding the many decisions involved in analyzing qualitative data—from how to code the data to how to incorporate theory—would take our discussion well beyond the bounds of what one short book can address.[49]

Still, we also recognize that we cannot fully avoid discussing analysis. A finished article or book will necessarily reflect analytical decisions, and because many qualitative projects involve an iterative movement between data collection and analysis, such decisions will often affect both the quality of the data and methods of collection.[50] For example, many ethnographers will spend a year in the field, analyze their data, and realize they need to return to the field for more data, which they then collect in more targeted fashion. In such cases, one cannot easily assess the methods of collection while ignoring the analytical approach. So, although our book centers largely on how to detect evidence of well-collected data, it must also address some aspects of qualitative analysis.

WHY WE ADDRESS IN-DEPTH INTERVIEWING AND PARTICIPANT OBSERVATION JOINTLY. The main reason we discuss them jointly is that the two methods share an important trait. To be sure, the methods are as different from each other as either of them is from, say, running an experiment or conducting a survey. A good interviewer is an effective listener, skilled at getting anyone to talk; in contrast, a good ethnographer is an acute observer, skilled at detecting elements of what places look, sound, smell, or feel like that others might miss. Some ethnographers will bristle at our plan of discussing quality in their work jointly with that of interviewers, and vice versa. The data each set of researchers collects—transcripts and field notes—differ dramatically in kind, and it would seem odd to identify standards common to both. And in fact the standards differ: in each of the chapters of this book, we separate the discussions of interviewing and ethnographic observation.

But the two methods share something uniquely consequential. What they share is not merely that interviewers and ethnographers often collect their own data. Experimenters typically collect their own data, too, as do all researchers who run their own surveys. Moreover, it is not merely that fieldwork requires care in managing personal bias, because that problem is common to all methods of data collection. For example, since surveys only elicit answers to questions the researcher decided to ask, they will necessarily reflect the researcher's interests, perspective, and predilections.

Instead, what interviewing and participant observation distinctly share is that the researcher not only collects but also *produces* the data, such that the data collector is explicitly in the data themselves.[51] Because an open-ended interview is a reactive interaction—in which the interviewer changes the wording, order, form, and content of what they ask or say in each interview in response to what the respondent says or does not say—the interviewer's own words, which will vary from interview to interview, are part of the data to be analyzed. Participant observation is also a reactive interaction, as even the most passive researcher, merely by being present, inevitably shapes what is observed. And given that the ethnographer writes every one of the hundreds of thousands of words that constitute a typical set of field notes, the observer is inescapably embedded in the data themselves.

When collecting either in-depth interview or observational data, researchers react in real time to the events before them; they ask or fail to ask questions in response to what was uttered, they direct their attention toward or away from some specific aspect of the event unfolding before them, and they decide whether and how to record the events they observe. These unpredictable reactions constitute a central component of the resulting data. If two in-depth interviewers with the same question guide were to interview separately the same person, they would produce different data (as long as the interview is open ended), because they would respond differently to what the participant says, ask different follow-up questions, and generally make different in-the-moment decisions about what to ask or comment on and how to do so.[52] If two ethnographers were to observe the same site at the same time with the same questions in mind, they would produce different field notes, because the ethnographers would differ on which of the infinite number of interactions, utterances, sights, sounds, smells, and other aspects of the site they would include and which they would deliberately exclude or unwittingly miss.[53] To be clear, any two interviewers or observers, with enough exposure, can arrive at the same fundamental social facts about a set of people or a field site. But their actual data—the resulting transcripts or field notes—will look dramatically different.

This expectation, that the very data collected will, by design, depend on the in-the-moment decisions of the data collector, creates unique challenges for a set of methods aiming to contribute to a cumulative social science, since the latter requires clear standards to determine data quality, and those standards have traditionally been based on collection rules one can set ahead of time, not on decisions made by the researcher while out in the field. Consider a contrast: if, in a given survey-based project, two research assistants administering the same instrument to the same respondent produced dramatically different responses, then that data collection process would be fundamentally flawed. Indeed, a base definition of reliability in survey or experimental data collection involves the expectation that there be no such (systematic) differences. Yet in any paired case of in-depth interviews or participant observations, such differences would be expected, because the researcher must make in-the-moment decisions that cannot be fully anticipated and must ultimately be part of the resulting data.[54]

Within Methods, Craft in Execution

Since the in-the-moment decisions of the researcher determine the quality of the data, a particular kind of craft is especially important to the data collection process. To make clear the kind of craft we are referring to, we must distinguish, within the process of data collection, between conception and execution. The former refers to the design process before data collection has started—whether those interviewed will be thought of as a sample or cases, whether a study will have many or few respondents, whether they will be interviewed repeatedly or just once, whether it will focus on a single or multiple field sites, and so forth. The latter refers to the actions of the researcher while actually collecting data, the practice of asking questions and observing others in real time. Conception happens in the office; execution, in the field. This book is primarily concerned with execution, where, regardless of design, the craftsmanship of the researcher is instrumental to the quality of the data.

WHY WE DO NOT FOCUS ON CONCEPTION. We do not focus on how data collection is conceived because doing so would require its own book. One reason is that the design process has many dimensions, including how many people are interviewed, for how long, how they are selected, whether one or multiple field sites are selected, how often they are observed, in what capacity, and many others. The range of additional issues we would need to cover is much too broad.

A second reason is the large number of disagreements over not only which design approaches are optimal but also whether some design decisions should be observed by all qualitative projects. Some qualitative researchers believe, inspired by survey research, that all interview-based studies should have large samples for which respondents are selected at random. Other researchers believe, inspired by experiments, that all ethnographic studies should include a comparison (or "control") site or group. In fact, one of the most controversial works in qualitative design proposed that criteria developed to collect survey data should be applied when collecting qualitative data, criteria that involve matters such as sample size, selection with known probability, sampling bias, and the like.[55]

We happen to disagree with the propositions that either survey or experimental data collection principles should inform qualitative data collection, that interview studies must have large samples, or that ethnographies must have multiple sites. One easy point of evidence is the work: many of the most important and distinguished qualitative studies over the last century focused on a handful of respondents or a single group, organization, research site, or event.[56] Different research objectives call for different designs, and sometimes small samples and single-site studies are called for. But making our case, and evaluating all the reasons researchers have offered for why their particular designs should be universal, is impossible within the confines of our short book.[57] As we will see, these disagreements do not affect the present discussion, because beliefs about conception need not translate into beliefs about execution.

Still, we must address one broad principle involving how design is conceived, because it affects language, the terms we use throughout the book to describe quality. Our perspective is that *all methods are effective to the extent they do what the methods are optimal for, not to the extent they emulate what other methods are optimal for.* Large-sample surveys are optimal means to accurately describe a large population; experiments, to precisely determine the effects of a cause in a controlled setting; participant observation, to directly observe phenomena in their natural contexts; and in-depth interviews, to elicit explicitly how people understand themselves and their circumstances. The techniques required to effectively perform each task differ dramatically from those needed to perform others.

By extension, each task calls for its own evaluation criteria. For example, we believe that while a sufficiently large sample is essential for an effective survey, that characteristic is perfectly fine for a high-quality interview study but not *essential* to it. Similarly, while an adequately selected comparison group—that is, control group—is indispensable for an effective experiment, it is not essential for an effective ethnography. Just as we would not fundamentally assess a laboratory experiment by whether participants were selected with known probability from a large population, and just as we would not fundamentally assess a survey by whether respondents were randomly assigned to a treatment, we also should not fundamentally assess open-ended interviewing or participant observation by criteria, or with language, immaterial to their core strengths. For these reasons, language such as "selection bias," "sampling bias," "variance," and "control group" will not form part of our discussion.[58]

Given the core strengths of in-depth interviewing, the method should be assessed primarily on whether the researcher effectively elicited how people understand themselves and their circumstances. Given the strengths of participant observation, it should be evaluated primarily on whether the ethnographer effectively observed social phenomena in their context. Our task in this book is to specify precisely what "effectively" means in each case.

WHY WE FOCUS ON CRAFT. Nevertheless, readers will not need to agree with our perspective on language—or to adopt any particular approach to research design or data analysis—to agree with the rest of the book, because these issues do not involve craft in execution. On quality in craft, we argue, there is little disagreement among experts, as is the case in many trades. Danish furniture makers may differ dramatically from Japanese *sashimono-shi* in how they approach, conceive of, and design a cabinet while clearly identifying craftsmanship in one another's work. Similarly, field-workers of different stripes routinely disagree over how to approach, conceive of, and design a project while still agreeing on signs of high craft in execution—in how an interviewer elicited data through conversation or how an ethnographer earned trust, captured context, and produced field notes.

Thus, this book's concern is not the many disagreements over either how to approach a project analytically or how to conceive it methodologically but the general points of agreement over craft in execution.

Finally, we stress that, in spite of our focus on craft, our goal is to offer not instruction on how to do fieldwork but rather guidance on how to evaluate it. We refer readers interested in learning how to conduct fieldwork to the numerous manuals in existence.[59]

The list of works in ethnographic observation is quite large and is supplemented by the methodological appendixes of many recent books.[60] The list of handbooks on interviews for social science methods is perhaps only somewhat smaller but is quite long as well and is also complemented by numerous methodological appendixes.[61] We also encourage researchers hoping to become effective field-workers to do the research, since the craft of collecting interview or observational data can only be learned through practice. But even without doing fieldwork, one can learn to identify quality when one sees it, just as one can come to appreciate exquisite Japanese joinery without ever laying hands on a saw.

What Follows

Each of the next five chapters presents one indicator we use to distinguish empirically well-executed from poorly executed data collection. We do not believe that only these five indicators typify good qualitative research, and we would expect other field-workers to be able to easily add to our list. Moreover, we do not believe that all good fieldwork must exhibit all five criteria, though we do find these five especially important and quite common in good research.

One Precondition: Exposure

Nevertheless, there is one precondition all good field projects possess. It is a high degree of what we call "exposure." The core advantage of both ethnographic observation and in-depth interviews is the direct contact each method has with the social world or its people. The greater the contact, the better the data. In interview research, exposure derives from the number of hours spent talking to respondents, and in-depth interviewers generally agree that more hours of interviewing lead to better data. In participant observation, exposure derives directly from the number of hours exposed to the field, and ethnographers generally agree that more time in the field produces better data.

Researchers do disagree on how to achieve that exposure. Survey-influenced interviewers believe that a large sample is a precondition for quality. But that belief is simply one interpretation of the idea of exposure, and not a necessary one. An interview study of 120 people interviewed for 1 hour will have far less exposure than one with 40 people interviewed four times each for 3 hours per interview. The first will have 120 hours of exposure; the second, 480. Interviewers from different perspectives will differ on which of the two approaches is preferable: some will insist that large samples are always better; others, that one-shot interviews are always suspect; and still others (like us), that which of the two is superior depends on the question. But they will certainly agree that, *ceteris paribus*, 480 hours of data are far more than 120, and that more data tend to yield greater *qualitative* insight about those who were interviewed. This difference helps explain why "sample size" turns out to be an unhelpful indicator of quality in interview research, while exposure, the more general idea, is actually not controversial.

Similarly, researchers from an experimental or comparative perspective may believe that studying multiple sites is a precondition for quality in an ethnography. But a study of four sites, each observed 20 hours a week for ten weeks, will have far less exposure than one of a single site observed 20 hours a week for eighteen months. The first will have 800 hours of exposure; the second,

1,560. Researchers will differ on which of the two approaches they prefer. But they will almost certainly agree that 1,560 hours of data are more than 800, and that more hours in a given field site will yield greater insight into what happens there. This difference, again, helps explain why the number of cases or field sites is rarely a helpful indicator of quality in ethnographic research, while greater total exposure is an idea that ethnographers generally support.

Thus, we posit that the core precondition of all good qualitative data is not "sample size" or "control groups" or "representativeness," all of which are necessary criteria for other methods, and all of which may be useful for some qualitative studies but not others; the core precondition of good qualitative data is exposure.

Five Indicators

Exposure is the foundation. But it is not a guarantee. The chapters that follow introduce what effective researchers can accomplish in the field—as they are producing the data—when they have sufficient exposure.

Chapter 1 examines "cognitive empathy," or the degree to which the researcher came to understand those observed close to how they understand themselves. This kind of understanding—about what people perceive, what it means to them, or what motivates them—is an objective of many qualitative studies, and the extent to which the field-worker has attained it depends directly on strategies employed when collecting data. The strategies in interviewing differ from those in participant observation, and we show the reader how to detect those strategies in the finished products of each. In this and the subsequent four chapters, we illustrate the strategies with hypothetical cases and then provide examples from published studies.

Chapter 2 focuses on "heterogeneity," or the extent to which the people or places depicted are represented as diverse. One of the consequences of high exposure is the ability to see differences one previously could not; in fact, this ability is one signal that a researcher has come to attain cognitive empathy. We show that, among both interview-based and participant observation studies, those that uncover little or no heterogeneity are ultimately unconvincing.

Chapter 3 centers on "palpability," or the degree to which the evidence presented is not abstract but concrete. What "palpable" evidence looks like depends, again, on whether the project is interview based or observational, but in both types of work, highly palpable evidence brings the reader close to what the participants actually experience. When evidence is not palpable, as we shall see, a finished work is distinctly less empirically grounded.

Chapter 4 focuses on "follow-up," or the extent to which the researcher collected data to answer questions that arose during the data-collection process itself. Gathering additional data to answer unanticipated questions is a form of responding to the field and one means through which good fieldwork gets closer to the experiences of those interviewed or observed. Although field-workers cannot answer every unanticipated question they uncover in their work, high-quality studies almost always involve extensive follow-up.

Chapter 5 centers on a somewhat more general indicator, "self-awareness," which we nonetheless define narrowly as the extent to which the researcher understands the impact of their presence and assumptions on those interviewed or observed. As we noted earlier, a core predicament of interviewing and observation as data-collection methods is that the data are not just collected but produced, and the researcher is inevitably in the data themselves. Researchers differ in their awareness of the implications of this fact, and such awareness can be detected in how researchers write about their decisions in the field and in the ensuing empirical data.

Our conclusion returns to the broader issue animating this book, which is the need to clarify standards for the evaluation of qualitative research, particularly work that seeks to contribute to cumulative social science. Our case for cognitive empathy, heterogeneity, palpability, follow-up, and self-awareness is part of our attempt to both introduce indicators that a broad swath of researchers can agree on and articulate ideas that many of them already believe. While some of the language we use is new, experienced field-workers will recognize much of what we describe, as many of the issues discussed here are tacitly understood but rarely articulated. We assume that other field-workers could easily add to what we have done, offering indicators beyond the five we have listed here. We hope they do, since building on what we propose represents direct evidence of our broader claim, that empirically grounded, scientifically oriented field research is indeed indispensable to cumulative knowledge.

1 Cognitive Empathy

Because qualitative studies differ in what they intend to do, how they use theory, and how they analyze data, they will differ in how they approach evidence. Regardless of approach, however, effective field-based research almost always shows clear signs of cognitive empathy. Among the most important objectives of qualitative empirical research, cognitive empathy is the degree to which the researcher understands how those interviewed or observed view the world and themselves—from their perspective.[1]

A cognitively empathetic researcher is not only one who can report what others say, because such reports do not require that the researcher understand others' views from their perspective. A researcher can report someone's belief that abortion constitutes killing an already-started life without understanding how that person arrived at their particular belief, why other beliefs about abortion do not compel the person as this one does, what significance that belief carries, and more. As the example suggests, cognitive empathy, the ability to understand what another understands, is a matter of degree. The better a researcher empathizes, the more accurately the scholar can describe a person's views; reveal the meaning of those views to the person who holds them; account for their origins; explain how coherent, reflective, or consistent they are; anticipate the person's views about other matters; and convince the person that they have been understood.

We stress that empathy is not sympathy. As one of us has recently written, "The latter is the feeling of pity or sorrow for the troubles of another; the former . . . is the sense that another's predicament is understood as they understand it. One can understand why a coworker yelled at another during a meeting without necessarily feeling sorry for the coworker—for example, while still believing he was rude. That understanding merely reflects the ability to see what another sees. Conversely, one can sympathize with a malnourished child in the midst of famine without understanding the sensation of prolonged hunger. Feeling pity does not require empathy."[2] Many field-workers are sympathetic to those they study. But whether they are or not is not an indicator of good empirical research. And many outstanding field-workers are not sympathetic to their respondents.[3]

Though the difference between empathy and sympathy may seem obvious, many published studies, and media accounts, use the former but mean the latter. In fact, as we discuss later, many empirical studies are ineffective because they communicate more sympathy than empathy, a feeling of solidarity with the position of those studied but not quite an understanding of how they see the world or why.

A researcher can cognitively empathize with many aspects of another's experience. Nonetheless, three are particularly important and will be our focus. The researcher may understand "perception," or how people see themselves or the social world; "meaning," or how they interpret what they see, say, or do; or "motivation," or what they express as the reasons behind their actions. While understanding perception is probably a bare minimum for good fieldwork, empirical studies will vary in how much they offer with respect to meaning or motivation. In what follows, we describe how a work may demonstrate that its author has come to understand those studied as they understand themselves. We begin with some background.

Background

Understanding from Others' Perspectives

The idea of putting oneself in the shoes of others has inspired thinkers throughout history. Adam Smith proposed that morality should be rooted in what he called "fellow-feeling," in "conceiving what ourselves should feel in [another person's] situation."[4] He believed that placing oneself in another's shoes is necessary to evaluate others' actions and thus is essential to moral behavior. George Herbert Mead believed it was even more important.[5] He argued that a necessary part of becoming a person—of understanding oneself as a "self"—is the ability to see oneself as if through the eyes of others: "The individual . . . enters his own experience . . . only in so far as he first becomes an object to himself just as other individuals are objects to him or in his experience; and he becomes an object to himself only by taking the attitudes of other individuals toward himself within a social environment or context of experience and behavior in which both he and they are involved."[6] In fact, for Mead the ability to put oneself in others' shoes was indispensable to complete self-fulfillment: "If the given human individual is to develop a self in the fullest sense . . . he must . . . , in the same way that he takes the attitudes of other individuals toward himself and toward one another, take their attitudes toward the various phases or aspects of the common social activity . . . which, as members of an organized society or social group, they are all engaged."[7]

This focus on understanding others was central to the budding science of society. Mead and others built on the notion of Verstehen, developed by nineteenth-century German thinkers to refer to the understanding of others.[8] Wilhelm Dilthey, for example, argued that what he called the "human sciences" would necessarily differ from the physical or natural sciences because human action is imbued with meaning, and meaning has to be interpreted to be understood.[9] Further, he believed that experiencing the lives of others was essential to this process: "The understanding [Verstehen] of other persons and their expressions of life is based upon the lived experience . . . and understanding of oneself, and their continual interaction."[10]

Perhaps the most influential thinker to conceptualize "understanding," in this sense, was Max Weber, who believed it to be foundational to social science. In the first section of the first chapter of the first volume of his *Economy and Society*, Weber argued that sociology as a science must first concern "itself with the interpretive understanding of social action," of any behavior in which people attach meaning to what they do and take account of the behavior of others.[11] For Weber, one of the core purposes of sociology is to understand the actions of others, and that understanding requires interpretation. As in Dilthey's model, understanding and interpretation went hand in hand for Weber, since the study of social action was, inevitably, the study of the meaning people give to their actions.

Perception, Meaning, and Motivation

The particular kind of "understanding" that Dilthey, Weber, and others refer to amounts to what we have called cognitive empathy. We have proposed that a qualitative researcher may, at a minimum, attain this kind of understanding about three things: perception, meaning, and motivation. The first, the foundation of any study in which cognitive empathy matters, is merely how others perceive themselves and the world around them.

Meaning is the significance people assign to what they see, think, say, or do. When researchers seek to understand meaning, they are reflecting the German Romantic idea that human actions and perceptions differ from those of other animals in that they are "meaningful" in the strict sense of the word.[12] As Clifford Geertz put it: "Believing, with Max Weber, that man is an animal suspended in webs of significance he himself has spun, I take culture to be those webs, and the analysis of it to be therefore not an experimental science in search of law but an interpretive one in search of meaning."[13] The aim is to understand what perceptions, actions, and statements mean to people. For example, a researcher may be concerned with understanding the significance that particular populations assign to marriage.[14]

Motivations are thornier. Weber describes a motive as "a complex of subjective meaning which seems to the actor himself or to the observer an adequate ground for the conduct in question."[15] Put differently, motivated actions are those an individual takes with a particular goal or outcome in mind. Since motives are themselves meaningful, part of understanding motivation is merely understanding the meaning people give to their actions, that is, how they interpret or account for what they have done.[16] But it also involves understanding what people believe led them to act in particular ways. Not all actions are motivated in the sense that people perceive them as goal driven or intentional; many are reactive, unreflective, habitual, or otherwise not motivated in any substantive sense. Thus, attaining cognitive empathy with respect to an action may imply understanding what it meant, that it meant nothing, what motivated it, or that it was not explicitly motivated at all.[17]

Moreover, even among motivated actions, to understand what motivated someone to commit an act is not equivalent to understanding its causes. First, the ultimate causes may lie well beyond the perception, understanding, or even experience of the individual. While motives are always immediate to the action, causes need not be proximate; they may be distal.[18] Second, actions may have multiple motives. It is possible for a person's account of their own motives to be only part of the whole story. Capturing some of these requires cognitive empathy; capturing others may require other methods or techniques.

Perception, meaning, and motivation share the fact that they cannot be observed directly. The researcher must elicit them through interviews or else attempt to infer them from behavior. Moreover, neither perception, meaning, nor motivation can be captured fully or perfectly, which is why cognitive empathy is necessarily a matter of degree. But researchers can, in fact, capture them more or less effectively. And just as the researcher must interpret a participant's perceptions, meanings, and motivations through that participant's statements or actions, an evaluator must assess the field-worker's effectiveness through the written work. In what follows, we show how, beginning with interview-based research.

Cognitive Empathy in In-Depth Interviewing

The interviewer's data are transcripts. The interviewer concerned with cognitive empathy can only communicate such understanding explicitly to the extent that it is present in the data—that is, to the extent the interviews themselves probed perception, meaning, or motivation. And whether the interviewer did so is readily detectable to anyone who knows what to look for. We begin with perception.

Perception

A hypothetical example will help guide our discussion. Consider the following passage:

> Seventeen-year-old Maria lived in a predominantly black, high-poverty neighborhood in Philadelphia. She explained, "I don't like my neighborhood, and I can't wait to get out. My school counselor says that my grades are good enough to get me into Penn State, but I have to do well on the SAT to get a scholarship. I can't wait."

The passage is a perfectly reasonable description of a teenager's thoughts about her neighborhood. However, it reflects a weak understanding of Maria's views as she sees them. Either the researcher could not empathize—again, regardless of whether they sympathized—with Maria's perceptions, or they otherwise chose not to present the data.

Suppose the researcher were only interested in understanding one aspect of perception, in how Maria sees her neighborhood. From the passage, we do not know at all what Maria perceives in her neighborhood. Because the neighborhood is predominantly black and high poverty, one can easily imagine many scenarios, but those scenarios would be the product of one's imagination, not of the data. What is worse, they would likely be informed by other studies, movies, stereotypes, and the like—none of which bear any necessary relationship to Maria's neighborhood.[19] A decent interviewer would, at a minimum, have asked her.

> Seventeen-year-old Maria lived in a predominantly black, high-poverty neighborhood in Philadelphia. She explained, "I don't like my neighborhood." I asked, "You don't? How come?" "It's gross. And I can't stand the people. I can't wait to get out."

The passage represents a step in the direction of greater cognitive empathy. The researcher, and now the reader, understand that Maria dislikes at least two aspects of the neighborhood: its physical appearance and the people who inhabit it. We also know at least one meaning she attributes to the neighborhood—grossness (more on this later).

Yet we still do not understand much. One way to know that we do not understand the neighborhood as she does is that we cannot quite picture what she pictures. Images, representations of spaces, people, or cultural objects, are essential to perception. Since "gross" and "people" can be pictured in many different ways, we can imagine many possibilities—but we do not know whether our picture matches hers. A stronger interviewer would, at a minimum, have asked explicitly.

> Seventeen-year-old Maria lived in a predominantly black, high-poverty neighborhood in Philadelphia. She explained, "I don't like

my neighborhood." I asked, "You don't? How come?" "It's gross."
"What makes it gross?" "Isn't it obvious? People throw garbage
all over the place, and the city only comes, like, once a month to
pick it up. And there's stupid graffiti everywhere, like, stupid gang
symbols—like, whatever, nobody cares about your stupid posse.
And people don't cleanup their stoops, so, there's always crap all
over the sidewalk. They throw barbeques and don't cleanup, just
leaving all the foil all over the place. And it smells like piss—sorry,
urine—on that block by the bus stop. I can't stand the people. And
I can't wait to get out. My school counselor says that my grades are
good enough to get me into Penn State."

The reader now has a much better understanding—a clearer
picture—of what Maria perceives. This understanding is possible
because, in the interview itself, the interviewer did not presume to
understand what they might not understand.

In the preceding passage, we have assumed, for the purpose
of our discussion, that the interviewer did not conduct participant
observation. But from the perspective of an effective interview,
that would not matter to the question at hand. Even if the interviewer had spent a year in the neighborhood, having an opinion
about what is gross is not synonymous with understanding why
Maria finds it gross.

Meaning

The interview not only elicited a clearer picture of what Maria
perceives; it also captured the meaning she attributed to it. Before, we had heard the term "gross" but did not know what she
meant by it. One can understand grossness in the abstract, and we

did, without understanding what characteristics of a neighborhood an individual finds gross. Now we comprehend that Maria was repulsed by the garbage, graffiti, barbeque leftovers, and urine.

Note that this understanding of the meaning she attributes to the term, and the neighborhood, does not depend on the researcher's, or reader's, agreement with the assessment, because our objective is to empathize, not sympathize—to understand her perceptions and the meanings she attaches to them, not to agree or disagree. Certainly most would probably express repulsion at the smell of human waste, yet others might have attached different meaning to the other physical attributes of the neighborhood that Maria described as "gross." The researcher, for example, might have found the graffiti colorful or imaginative, rather than stupid, and the sight and smell of barbeques as reminiscent of family and community, rather than something to eschew. What matters for cognitive empathy is neither the ostensibly obvious nor the most common nor the researcher's interpretation of a set of attributes—only the respondent's.

Motivation

In the very first passage, the interviewer reported Maria's motive for wanting to leave her neighborhood: "I don't like my neighborhood." But the passage offered only a thin understanding of that motivation. In the very last passage, we had a better sense of Maria's motives, because we understood what she did not like about the neighborhood. Yet that passage, which reflects that the researcher wanted to understand Maria's perceptions and what they meant to her, demonstrates only minimal insight into the motives behind her desire to leave the neighborhood.

Consider how a researcher concerned with fully understanding motivation might have approached the tail end of Maria's statement. The interviewer likely would have asked additional questions about her motives.

"And it smells like piss—sorry, urine—on that block by the bus stop. I can't stand the people. And I can't wait to get out." "Get out? How come?," I asked. "Huh? Isn't it obvious? I mean, did you hear what I just said?" "Well, do your friends who hate the neighborhood want to get out, too?" "Yeah, obviously, they all do. I mean, well, the boys always say they'll 'never leave the hood' but they're stupid. And one of my girlfriends says she doesn't want to do college right away, and wants to stick around to 'help the community' or whatever until she figures out what to do. But I think that's just because she flunked trig and English last year."

The interviewer did something important, which was to not presume that a particular perception necessarily implied a motive to act. By openly asking whether others with the same perception of the neighborhood also wanted to get out, the interviewer created an opening to understand motivations more clearly. This particular technique is to respond to an expressed motive by asking about plausible alternatives. It can be extended further.

"So, if you had failed some courses do you think you wouldn't want as much to get out?" "Thing is, I know I want to go to college. My moms had me at, like, seventeen, and I'm not about to repeat that. Hell no. I have to go to college. My school counselor says that my grades are good enough to get me into Penn State, but I have to do well on the SAT to get a scholarship. I can't wait."

This technique, counterfactual questioning, is only one approach to eliciting motives.[20] There are others.[21] Still, note that the interviewer did not presume that Maria's aspirations to get out have a single motive. Probing motivation further in one or another way provides a much clearer understanding of what Maria sees as her motives for wanting to leave her neighborhood. Her aspirations derive, at a minimum, from her displeasure with her neighborhood, the fear of repeating her mother's experience, and the opportunities afforded to her by her academic success.

You will note that the last passage, taken in full, is much longer than the first. When interviewers seek cognitive empathy, interviews can take many hours. And reporting effective interviews, to represent cognitive empathy, requires space, the ability to exhibit the evidence that the interviewer asked the right questions at the right time.

Note also that the passage, even the extended version, only tapped into how one person understood one neighborhood and the implications of that perception. The more complex the questions, the more space the interviewer would have needed to demonstrate that they had come to understand how the respondents understand themselves. This need for space is part of the reason many of the strongest interview-based studies tend to be reported in books, rather than papers, and why the interview-based studies that appear in papers are often necessarily narrow in scope.

An Example

Many of the best interview-based studies reflect a high level of cognitive empathy—it is clear from the text that the researchers came to understand their participants close to how their participants understood themselves.[22] An example is Celeste Watkins-Hayes's study of women living with HIV, many of whom were African American.[23] The phrase "black woman with HIV," much like "person who thinks abortion should be illegal," invokes a number of images and stereotypes—about what they look like, how they see the world, what their income is, how they vote, and even what kind of environment they live in. These stereotypes are informed by media accounts, journalism, and even past research, and are a threat to the serious researcher hoping to understand people impartially.[24] Studying such populations requires care that the researcher's beliefs, whether positive or negative, sympathetic or antagonistic, do not get in the way of understanding the persons studied as they see themselves.

Watkins-Hayes, a highly skilled interviewer, steers clear of such dangers and gives us that understanding. Consider her discussion of Dawn, a now middle-aged woman diagnosed with HIV in 1985 at age twenty-four. Watkins-Hayes begins with a startling quote from Dawn: "If it weren't for HIV, I'd probably be dead."[25] The statement makes the reader to want to ask: What would make someone say that?

For her project, Watkins-Hayes attained an extraordinary amount of exposure, interviewing Dawn and many other women over the span of ten years, and it is impossible to recount her full analysis here. However, central to Watkins-Hayes's answer is the idea that the HIV safety net provided Dawn and other women with more robust resources than they might otherwise have accessed, including housing, support groups, therapy, case management, access to health care, and the opportunity to use her voice politically to make change.

The HIV safety net gave Dawn an escape from the difficulties she had experienced prior to her diagnosis. Consider the many private, painful, and even humiliating aspects of her life Dawn confided in Watkins-Hayes. Dawn was a victim of sexual trauma inflicted by several relatives before age sixteen; she succumbed to serious drug abuse throughout much of her late teens, twenties, and thirties; she became a street sex worker in a high-risk context, ending up in and out of jail for several years; she faced homelessness many times, eventually making more than fifty residential moves as an adult; and she tried many times unsuccessfully before middle age to stay clean. While making a living in the streets, she had seen many other sex workers victimized: "I saw a woman dragged by a car. I've seen women get beaten and raped. While I was out there, I refused to be one of those women."[26] At age thirty-one, "Dawn was arrested for knifing a customer who attempted to sexually assault her."[27] At the penitentiary, in 1992, she was again informed of her diagnosis, which given her state of mind at the time failed to make much impact on her thinking. After her release, she entered a course-mandated education program where she began to learn about the seriousness of her illness. Things would get much worse, with severe addiction to hard drugs, an increase in behavior as a sex worker risky to herself and others, and the experience of having each of her four children removed by social services. Dawn asked for no sympathy.

Her life would only begin to turn around after a stint at a housing facility for women with HIV, where she began to acquire the psychological, medical, and institutional tools to make a lasting change. She met a fellow resident also in recovery and fell in love, learning a great deal about her sexuality and healthier forms of intimacy. Dawn's time in the housing facility, lasting two years, transformed how she saw herself, related to her family, and maintained her health. Her viral load is now undetectable.

The many aspects of her life that Dawn recounted to Watkins-Hayes make clear that she trusted the researcher. That trust helps the reader trust the researcher as well. Even in the brief discussion excerpted here we learn a lot about Dawn's perception, meaning, and motivation. For example, we learn how she perceived her sex work (as dangerous, and at times a source of power) and how and why; we learn what her HIV diagnosis meant to her (the first two times, in 1985 and in 1992, nearly nothing); and we learn what motivated the knifing that landed her in jail at age thirty-one (her refusal to be a victim). Given what Watkins-Hayes communicated to readers, we know that the author attained a deep level of cognitive empathy, because we begin to attain it as well. We understand that without the HIV safety net, Dawn—low-income, alone, homeless, in and out of jail, and grappling with substance abuse—would have had difficulty making it to thirty-five. But the facility was only open to women who had been diagnosed with HIV. So, yes, for this and other reasons—there is much more in the book—we begin to understand why Dawn could believe that HIV, and more specifically the HIV safety net it gave her access to, had come to save her life.

Cognitive Empathy in Participant Observation

The majority of ethnographers who spend time in neighborhoods, organizations, villages, or other spaces also interview locals as part of their work. In that respect, all of the issues previously discussed are relevant. In fact, seeking cognitive empathy will often require the researcher to listen to people speak in their own words.[28] But for the moment we focus strictly on the observational aspect of research, wherein the data at one's disposal are not interview transcripts but the observer's field notes. How do field notes communicate cognitive empathy?

Perception

In contrast to the interviewer, the observer must seek to understand what people perceive not by asking but through direct experience, by observing spaces, people, and the relationship between the two. Such experience can bring advantages, including not needing to rely on others' representations. At the same time, observations constitute an entirely different kind of data.

Recall the first few sentences of the passage with which we started: "Seventeen-year-old Maria lived in a predominantly black, high-poverty neighborhood in Philadelphia. She explained, 'I don't like my neighborhood, and I can't wait to get out.'" Now suppose that, as before, the researcher was interested in the young woman's perception of the neighborhood. And suppose—only for the sake of this discussion—that the researcher had no interview data, no opportunity to talk to her. A decent researcher concerned with perception might report what the woman perceived.

> She stepped off the bus. Heading north, she tiptoed around barbeque leftovers on the sidewalk—foil, charcoal, a few paper plates. As she crossed the street, she saw two men in their early twenties spraying graffiti on the brick wall of a corner townhouse.

While the researcher did not interview this person, they have a reasonable sense of some of what she perceived. Indeed, the researcher did many things well, including describing concrete events as they took place and giving us a picture of what she saw (see chapter 3).

But there are two limitations. First, while we know what the woman saw, we do not know what the researcher saw. For example, we have no idea what this person the researcher has described looks like. Since we do not know much about what the researcher saw or experienced, we have little basis to know whether the researcher, as observer, attained the ability to perceive the neighborhood as the woman perceived it. Second, we have only a superficial understanding of what the woman saw. Perception involves not just sight but all the senses—smell, touch, taste, and sound—since everything that can be sensed affects how one perceives one's surroundings.

Addressing both issues would lead to much better data. For example, recall from earlier that Maria hated the smell of the neighborhood. A better observer who was interested in capturing, and communicating, that they understood what this woman they were observing perceived might have written the following:

In a predominantly black, high-poverty neighborhood in Philadelphia, a woman who appeared to be in her late teens stepped off a bus, wearing a blue-and-white school uniform, a school bag slung over her shoulder. She had dark brown skin and a large Afro. Heading north, she tiptoed around barbeque leftovers on the sidewalk—foil, charcoal, a few paper plates. It was a crisp September afternoon; a plane roared overhead. As she crossed the street, she saw two men in their early twenties spraying graffiti on the brick wall of a corner townhouse. Both wore fitted black pants, high-top sneakers, and oversized sweaters. By the end of the block, near another bus stop, she stared at a dark yellow stain on the pavement— the block smelled of urine.

The author has given us a picture of the woman, with enough detail to help us understand how the author came to believe that the woman who stepped off the bus was in high school. The author also has given us a sense of what the place looked, sounded, and smelled like. As readers, we can now perceive the place much more clearly, which allows us to understand what the young woman saw and to believe that the observer has attained some level of understanding with respect to the woman's perceptions. Without making evaluative judgments, the author has provided us with a great deal of data. Naturally, the more we can perceive, the more we understand.

Meaning

Depicting the meaning behind observed action is what Geertz referred to as "thick description."[29] Geertz was making the case that anthropologists should devote themselves to studying not structure but culture, to focus specifically on the meanings that people give their circumstances. He used the term "thick description" to define the kind of descriptive research in which the objective was to uncover people's meanings. Many contemporary scholars treat "thick description" as synonymous with "rich" or "detailed" description. But while greater detail is often good for ethnographic data, richly detailed description is not, by itself, thick description. In fact, thick description need not be especially detailed. The point of thick description is to describe meaning—what words, symbols, interactions, or cultural objects mean to people—not just to describe their life in a lot of detail.

Reconsider the preceding passage. Though it gives us a reasonably detailed picture of what the observed woman perceived, it offers us nothing on what those perceptions meant to her. The high school student could have been totally fine with what she saw, rather than disgusted. She could have been happy about the graffiti, as would be the case, for example, if the art were gang related and she were affiliated with the gang. Or she could have been indifferent to all of it. Depending on the study's aims, understanding what the student's neighborhood meant to her may or may not be important. But we must be clear that understanding meaning is a distinct objective, and describing effectively what people perceive is not synonymous with describing what it means to them.

How do we uncover meaning? Whereas the interviewer can ask, the observer who does not ask people what things mean to them must rely on other tools. Probably the two most important involve interaction: people's interactions with their spaces and with one another. Interactions can provide powerful clues about what spaces, people, or cultural objects mean to others. Consider the following passage:

In a predominantly black, high-poverty neighborhood in Philadelphia, a woman who appeared to be in her late teens stepped off a bus, wearing a blue-and-white school uniform, a school bag slung over her shoulder. Heading north, she tiptoed around barbeque leftovers on the sidewalk—foil, charcoal, a few paper plates—while shaking her head, a grimace on her face. It was a crisp September afternoon; a plane roared overhead. As she crossed the street, she saw two men in their early twenties spraying graffiti on the brick wall of a corner townhouse. Both wore fitted black pants, high-top sneakers, and oversized sweaters. They were laughing. She shook her head again. "You guys are stupid—that doesn't even look good!" "Shut up, Maria! Mind your business!" "You shut up! *Hijo 'e puta!*" By the end of the block, near another bus stop, she held her nose while staring at a dark yellow stain on the pavement—the block smelled of urine—and shook her head once more.

We now have two powerful types of data that allow us to infer meaning. From her interactions with her surroundings—her shaken head and grimace at the leftovers and the urine stain—we have a better sense of what her perceptions meant to her. From her interactions with the two men—what she said to them and how—we know something of her thoughts about the graffiti and about the men spraying it on the wall. By paying careful attention to her interactions with other people and her surroundings, the observer can reasonably infer a lot about meaning even without recourse to the interview. And by including such accounts in the field notes, the researcher can help the reader understand what the observer understood.[30]

Motivation

Capturing what people believe their motives to be is best done through interviews.[31] But several aspects of motive can be observed as well. In Maria's case, the researcher can observe how often she goes to tutoring classes and SAT prep and reasonably infer how strongly motivated she is to go to college. The researcher can observe her attending school sessions on safe sex and taking advantage of free prophylactics offered at the sessions and reasonably infer that she is strongly motivated to avoid pregnancy. The researcher can observe how she talks to peers during lunch hour and what she says about getting out of the neighborhood and infer that her disgust contributes to her motives. Whether observing these actions would offer more insights into motivation than just asking depends on the objectives of the project. But observation is a powerful tool.

An Example

While ethnographers often rely on interviews, we focus our example on field-note data. Skilled ethnographers can communicate much of what they have come to understand by mere use of their field notes. Consider Andrew Deener's recent study of ethnic and class conflict in Venice, California.[32] Deener studied the neighborhood for at least five years, attended "over 150 community meetings, festivals, protests, and other events," and interviewed informally a large number of residents and others about their lives and neighborhoods, attaining a very high level of exposure.[33] While an ethnographer who has spent sufficient time in a field site inevitably comes to understand a lot about how its people see themselves, mere exposure is insufficient—if the researcher fails to probe, observe carefully, write good field notes, or take note of telling events, they will often only arrive at, and convey, a rather superficial level of cognitive empathy.

Deener, by contrast, demonstrated a high level of cognitive empathy. We cannot do full justice to the book in these pages. However, some examples will make clear how Deener convinced the reader that residents perceived themselves to be living in a neighborhood facing ethnic conflict. He described a series of events.

As I sit in the kitchen of my Venice apartment . . . reading a book, a deafening roar shakes the floors and walls, jarring me out of my concentration. At first, I am unsure if these are signs of an earthquake. The vibrations and racket continue, and I cautiously open the front door. . . . I notice the shadow of a helicopter on the ground, and when I look up, one is flying so low that I can feel the breeze that it gives off and clearly read the letters L-A-P-D as it circles around.[34]

The helicopter, he later learned, was looking for a shooter described as an "African American male teenager" following the death of a "male Hispanic student" near the campus of the Venice High School.[35] Black men throughout the neighborhood were targeted. Deener recounted his conversations with neighbors.

Lakesha Holt, an African American resident, said that she was at work and saw her house on television. She watched police officers rappel out of helicopters onto her roof and surround her house on all sides with guns drawn in search of her nephew whom they believed fit the description, despite the fact that the alleged shooter is seventeen and her nephew is in his thirties.[36]

That same evening, it so happened that a councilman had planned a community meeting to "address issues stemming from race and class tensions."[37] At the meeting of "approximately one hundred people . . . about 70 percent were" black; there were "fewer than ten Latinos," and the remainder were white.[38] During the meeting, Deener saw many black men step to the podium. "One after another, they call[ed] attention to the emotional scars [of being] . . . beaten and harassed by police officers."[39]

In recounting these events, Deener did a number of things well. First, rather than describing ethnic conflict in general terms, he focused on a concrete incident that showed some of the many ways conflict manifested itself—for example, as an interethnic shooting and as racial profiling by police. Second, as we recommended earlier in our hypothetical example, Deener made clear how he knew what he purported to know. We know his place in his narrative— he was at home, in the neighborhood, beneath the helicopter, and later at the meeting—and therefore we can assess the grounds for what he is reporting. Third, to describe what he observed, Deener made use of multiple senses. He told us what things looked like (e.g., the helicopter was low enough that he could read its lettering), sounded like (e.g., it was loud, roaring), and felt like (e.g., the earthquake-like vibrations, the breeze). Fourth, he showed us how residents came to perceive their own neighborhood as they did— that is, he described to us what they saw. Just as we learned that the young woman in our example saw two men spraying graffiti while walking down the street, Deener told us that Lakesha herself saw several officers rappel onto her house on television. Finally, by describing people's reactions to their events (e.g., the comments at the meetings), he made clear what the events meant to them, providing clear evidence for his larger claim, that those he was observing believe there to be ethnic conflict.

These techniques illustrate how an effective ethnographer can communicate cognitive empathy with respect to not only perception but also meaning and motivation. Deener showed that he perceived some of what they perceived. He showed that this military-style surveillance did not mean nothing, but was instead upsetting to many black men because they stood up at a podium to express the fact. And he showed that the councilman was motivated to organize the meeting by the ethnic conflict not only because that is what he announced as his motivation but also because that is what residents discussed at the meeting itself. These and other techniques were deployed repeatedly throughout the book, by the end of which the reader is convinced that Deener could cognitively empathize with those he studied.

Conclusion

Cognitive empathy is a central feature of strong qualitative research. We stress that cognitive empathy is a matter of degree. No researcher can fully occupy the figurative shoes of those studied, but the careful researcher can get much closer than others, and getting closer is indispensable to good qualitative science.

2 Heterogeneity

We have argued that the most important precondition of good qualitative work is exposure, the amount of time the researcher has spent with those interviewed or observed. Exposure does a lot for the researcher, including building rapport with those studied, generating trust, increasing cognitive empathy, and expanding the range of issues about the people or context that the researcher comes to understand. It also increases the researcher's overall sensitivity to subtleties in speech and action that would have been missed at the start of the study.

In the finished narrative, one can detect this sensitivity when depictions exhibit high heterogeneity, which we define as the degree to which the perceptions, experiences, motivations, and other aspects of the population or context studied are represented as diverse. Though interview-based and ethnographic works depict heterogeneity differently, across both kinds of research it is nonetheless a consistent sign of quality. Effective qualitative works tend to depict people and places that are far more diverse than a newcomer to those studied might have expected—even if the study involves people from a single field site or demographic group.

Background

Producing a narrative that depicts heterogeneity is neither simple nor inevitable. As psychologists have shown, people are subject to out-group homogeneity bias—individuals' tendency to think of the groups they are part of as more diverse or heterogeneous than those to which they do not belong.[1] We can easily detect the differences in beliefs, attitudes, physical appearances, orientation, taste, context, and environment in members of our own groups, but have great, at times enormous, difficulty detecting these in other groups. This blindness to diversity can manifest itself in any context wherein the observer is of a group different from the observed. It can be seen in political views, as when Democrats tend to see Republicans as homogeneous ("they're all racist anti-immigrants") and vice versa ("they're all radical socialists").[2] It can be seen with respect to facial features, as when whites from racially homogenous environments have difficulty detecting the differences between black faces, and vice versa.[3] Recent psychological research suggests that people even process information about in-groups differently from that about out-groups, with the latter mental action involving less refinement.[4] As a result of out-group homogeneity bias, anyone studying a population or context different from themselves or their environment is, at least initially, bound to see those studied as a fairly homogeneous lot.

But this bias need not be permanent. Research suggests that as familiarity increases, the part of the brain with which the actor processes information changes, too.[5] The more exposure a researcher has to the world of those studied, the more difference the researcher detects. The more hours over multiple sessions the interviewer spends with the respondent, the more the former can detect the contradictions, mood changes, shifts in opinions, and variations in perceptions in the latter. The more time an ethnographer spends at a field site, whether a large corporation or low-income neighborhood or high-performing school, the more differences the researcher detects in its members, its characteristics, and the fluctuations in both over time.

"Out-group homogeneity bias" is a psychological, not sociological or anthropological, term. It is not a term that either participant observers or interviewers typically use in their work or even discuss with others explicitly. Nor is one likely to find this notion, or its discussion, in most textbooks on how to conduct fieldwork. Yet experienced researchers regularly demonstrate sensitivity to the issue both implicitly and explicitly, because as they spend time in the field they inevitably become aware of heterogeneity in those studied that they were previously not privy to. Heterogeneity becomes an indicator of quality in data collection because detecting it is an inevitable result of sufficient attentive exposure; homogeneity in a narrative suggests the research was not sufficiently exposed or did not probe deeply enough.

It is important to note that depicting heterogeneity, as we are discussing it, is not synonymous with what social scientists sometimes mean by "examining variation." Heterogeneity is an indicator of good work because, as we shall see in detail, such work depicts the degree of diversity in people or contexts that insiders—members of a particular group or community—know there to be.[6] Some social scientists use the term "variation" to describe a feature of research design—of how data collection is conceived—believing that studies must be set up to include not one but multiple kinds of people, groups, study sites, or contexts before the study begins. We do not believe that this kind of variation (or the inclusion of explicit comparison groups) is necessary for a study to be empirically sound. For example, many outstanding ethnographies are based on research in a single neighborhood or organization.[7] Moreover, a study of a single site or group can still exhibit high heterogeneity. We use "heterogeneity" to describe not a feature of the research design but the character of the written report. As we shall see, when qualitative research, whether interview based or observational, is convincing, it almost always depicts heterogeneity among people or their contexts in one way or another.

Heterogeneity in In-Depth Interviewing

When an interviewer is highly exposed to those studied, either by spending many hours with interviewees or by interviewing many of them, two things inevitably happen. First, the interviewer begins to notice patterns, similarities across situations or across people in what they say about themselves, their circumstances, or others. Second, the interviewer notices differences—that is, differences across the people being observed on the questions at hand. Just as the person exposed long enough to a population ethnically different from themselves improves their ability to tell faces apart, and just as the person long enough in a country with a different language improves their ability to tell accents apart, so does the interviewer begin to notice differences that were entirely inaccessible before the research began.[8] The researcher studying reactions to undocumented status begins to realize how much such immigrants differ in the degree to which they fear prosecution.[9] The researcher interviewing rural conservatives begins to realize how much such voters differ in their opinions about nationalism.[10] The researcher studying gang members begins to realize how much such young people differ in their attitudes about violence.[11] The researcher interviewing unhoused people begins to realize how much they differ in how much they prefer the streets to a shelter.[12] With long enough exposure, uncovering heterogeneity is inescapable.

Good interviewers not only encounter this heterogeneity (by virtue of their exposure) but also take it seriously. How they do so, however, will depend on the relationship between the kind of heterogeneity they have uncovered and the empirical question they are answering. For our discussion, it is useful to distinguish interview studies, or sections of studies, in which the focus is primarily the individual and those in which the focus is primarily the group. As we shall see, research projects may depict heterogeneity in either unit of analysis.

The Individual

To some quantitative researchers—and even to interview researchers who primarily conduct large-sample studies—it may seem strange for an empirical, social scientific study to focus on the life of one or a small number of individuals. But digging deep into the experiences of the individual is essential to capturing their understanding of their circumstances, their experiences, and their motivations. In fact, many studies—both interview and observation based—that have dug deep into a handful of persons have proven crucial to both scholarship and the public interest. Annette Lareau's *Unequal Childhoods* and Matthew Desmond's *Evicted* both primarily told the stories of about a dozen families.[13] Jay MacLeod's classic *Ain't No Makin It*, now in its third edition, was based on two groups of about a half dozen teenagers.[14] Mario L. Small's *Villa Victoria* devoted an entire, extended chapter to discussing the lives of five individuals.[15] Mary Pattillo's *Black Picket Fences*, Nikki Jones's *The Chosen Ones*, and Celeste Watkins-Hayes's *Remaking a Life* each devoted similar chapters to a single person.[16] Clifford Shaw's entire book, the often-cited *The Natural History of a Delinquent Career*, was based on the criminal justice experiences of one young man.[17] Indeed, any readers who remember "Chick Morelli" in William Foote Whyte's *Street Corner Society*, or "Ruby Banks" in Carol Stack's *All Our Kin*, are experiencing what happens when skilled researchers report on the experiences of an individual with such care that the person is not easily forgotten.[18]

Thus, examining what happens when a researcher examines effectively the conditions of a single individual or small set of persons is instructive. With enough exposure to any individual, the researcher comes to see a great deal of heterogeneity, and this diversity can take many forms. For example, the person may have voted for different political parties in different elections or have had different beliefs over the course of their lives about when to prioritize work over family. The range of domains about which an interviewer could report diversity about a person is essentially infinite. Nevertheless, when books and articles have represented diversity among individuals, they have often done so about three issues: how the individual understands themselves or their circumstances, the nature of the experiences the individual has had around a given issue, or what the individual reports as the motivations behind their actions. We elaborate on all three.

To help our discussion, imagine a study in which the researcher is investigating, based on in-depth interviews, the personal networks of undocumented immigrants. The researcher, in a chapter centered on one individual, Sofia, reports that her networks were supportive.

> Sofia, who moved to New York without papers when she was nineteen, was embedded in a support network that provided information about jobs, help during emergencies, and emotional aid. She explained, in Spanish, "When I need something, I know I can turn to other people from my hometown. I got my cleaning job from my cousin, who told her boss about me."

The passage is perfectly reasonable. It makes a theoretical claim about Sofia and provides some evidence of that claim. It provides a concrete example. But if the chapter were based entirely on statements of this kind, all of them consistent with the claim that Sofia was or saw herself embedded in a network that provided information, help, and emotional support, then one or more conclusions would follow: the researcher did not get enough exposure, the researcher was exposed but did not probe effectively, the researcher probed carefully but chose to ignore heterogeneity, or the researcher noticed heterogeneity but chose to not report it. A sufficiently exposed researcher who probed carefully and reported accurately would have reported heterogeneity in at least one of the three forms we have described.

DEPICTING HETEROGENEITY OF UNDERSTANDING. One form is the understanding people have of themselves or their circumstances. In the passage, the author focused on Sofia's perception of herself and her circumstances, and we know that she has some understanding of herself as having other people she can turn to. But an effective researcher with this interest would likely have probed further, and such probing, with enough time and attention, would likely have uncovered heterogeneity.

She explained, in Spanish, "When I need something, I know I can turn to other people from my hometown. I got my cleaning job from my cousin, who told her boss about me."

"Have you always thought that about people from your hometown?" I asked.

"Well, not at the beginning. When I first moved to New York I didn't go to a lot of people. A lot of people did not help, maybe because they thought I didn't have much to give back. Or maybe because I didn't ask enough, I'm not sure."

"How have things changed?"

"Now I always ask. Anyone from my hometown. Well, some of them. There are two large families in the town back home that don't get along, and here I can't go to anyone on the Gutierrez-Ochoa side. So, I know them but we stay away from each other."

The interviewer explicitly asks more about how Sofia understands her network—specifically, if the belief that she can turn to people from her hometown has been a constant. We now see that her belief has varied over time, and varies from person to person (or across families). Our picture of her perception of her network incorporates more diversity—heterogeneity—and we understand her as a more complex individual. As you may recall from the previous chapter, when an interviewer probes deeper to seek cognitive empathy about perception, the resulting picture is often more heterogeneous.

DEPICTING HETEROGENEITY OF EXPERIENCE. A different way an interview study may reveal heterogeneity is in its depiction of the respondents' experiences themselves. Note that the first passage describes both Sofia's understanding of her circumstances ("I can turn to others") and her experience ("I got my job from my cousin"). Perception and experience are, naturally, related, but at times the researcher does not care much how people perceive—or, more broadly, understand—things, just what they have experienced. For example, a researcher may be interested in how people make ends meet while living on minimum wage, what people had to go through to cross the southern US border, how being open about their sexual orientation was received at work, or what aspects of their everyday life changed after a natural disaster.

Consider a researcher who cares deeply about what Sofia has experienced (and less about how she understands herself). After the preceding passage, the researcher would ask a different kind of follow-up question.

> She explained, in Spanish, "When I need something, I know I can turn to other people from my hometown. I got my cleaning job from my cousin, who told her boss about me."
>
> "Does your cousin often help that way?" I asked.
>
> "Not always. For several years she didn't help me, because at the first job she got me I made a mistake and got fired. We just fixed our relationship this year, after I was going through a difficult time."
>
> "Who helped you during that time?"
>
> "Well, my stepbrother wouldn't help me. My sister-in-law let me sleep on her couch for several months. Other than that, I am on my own."

This account of Sofia's experience paints a more heterogenous picture. The cousin has sometimes helped and sometimes not;

some family members would never help. Indeed, even if Sofia is embedded in a network that on the whole is supportive, we now see that the network does not always come through for every need. The account of Sofia's experience is far more believable, because it exhibits the heterogeneity we know to exist in real-world relationships. Pressure to report an uncomplicated story—or to write within strict word limits—can tempt researchers to either ignore or not pursue heterogeneity of experiences. But people's experiences surrounding any issue or topic can vary dramatically over their lifetimes or across situations, and a researcher who took care to probe the interviewee enough would surely capture this heterogeneity.

DEPICTING HETEROGENEITY OF MOTIVATIONS. A study can also reveal heterogeneity in its reports of people's motives for action, such as why people vote for whom they do, why they decide to opt out of the labor force, why they join gangs, or why they divorce. As we have noted in a previous chapter, any study of the motives behind action must proceed with special care.[19] The key issue here is that the effective interviewer is attuned to the fact that many actions are driven by multiple and even contradictory motives. If the respondent consistently expresses a single motive behind their actions, then something is probably amiss.

For an illustration, recall Maria, from our previous chapter. An uncritical interviewer would have moved on after hearing that she wanted to go to college because of her displeasure with her neighborhood. Just a bit of effective probing quickly unveiled at least one other motivation—her fear of repeating her mother's experience. As before, more exposure translates into greater diversity, in this case diversity of motivation, even within a single participant and with respect to a single choice.

THE RELATION BETWEEN EMPIRICAL HETEROGENEITY AND THEORETICAL CONCEPTS. Our discussion to this point has focused strictly on the interviewer's ability to accurately depict empirical facts: what people understand their circumstances to be, what their experiences of a particular kind have been, or how they represent their motivations. We have argued that, given the interview process, describing those facts well will tend to reveal a great deal of diversity or heterogeneity. But social science does not merely report empirical facts; it also connects those facts to theoretical concepts. And the researcher must be thoughtful about how to incorporate that heterogeneity when producing simplifying concepts or claims.

Recall the first passage with which we started: "Sofia, who moved to New York without papers when she was nineteen, was embedded in a support network that provided information about jobs, help during emergencies, and emotional aid. . . .'When I need something, I know I can turn to other people from my hometown. I got my cleaning job from my cousin.'" Note that the passage was not merely describing perception and experience; it was also introducing a theoretical concept, "embeddedness in a support network," to make a claim about what the respondent has experienced and why. That support network is proposed to provide job information, help during emergencies, and emotional aid. While this concept happens to be consistent with some theories about the lives of undocumented migrants in the United States, the original passage only provided meager evidence to suggest that Sofia's experience aligned with that concept or claim—Sofia had gotten job information from a member of her network. However, the author offered no evidence that they had probed further in this regard. Such probing often shows that the relationship between the concept and the evidence is not so straightforward, because of the diversity inherent in the real world.

To be clear, concepts such as "support network," by definition, must mask a lot of the heterogeneity in the world. But when researchers decide to ignore or not probe the heterogeneity of the empirical world for the sake of producing a single concept, they run the risk of undermining the confidence of the experienced reader, since, knowing that heterogeneity is common in the world, the reader has to wonder what was left out for the sake of the theory.

To illustrate a better alternative, we return to Sofia and present two examples based on different approaches to theory—one deductive, one inductive—of how heterogeneity might be reconciled with a theory about her networks. In both, the researcher is comfortable with some heterogeneity in the experience, and the reader, having seen it, accommodates it into our understanding of the simplifying concept.

One approach is deductive, in the sense that the researcher, before conducting the empirical research, already had the concept of "embedded in a support network" in mind and wants to determine whether the concept is consistent with Sofia's experience. A researcher testing the applicability of that concept to Sofia's case but sensitive to such heterogeneity might have reported the following:

Sofia, who moved to New York without papers when she was nineteen, was embedded in a support network. She explained, in Spanish, "When I need something, I know I can turn to other people from my hometown."

"What kind of needs can you turn to them for?" I asked.

"I got my cleaning job from my cousin, who told her boss about me."

"Do they help with other things, like when you have an emergency or need help talking through problems?"

"Definitely when I have emergencies. But I can't talk to them about personal things. It's not really appropriate."

The reader can see clearly that the overarching concept "support network" is simplifying a more complex reality. While Sofia's reality matches the concept that support networks provide job information and help during emergencies, it is not consistent with the idea that it also provides emotional aid. We better trust the author that they are not masking details for the sake of their theory.

Another approach is inductive, in the sense that the researcher has only a general question in mind but not an a priori concept and is thus developing, not testing, theory. An equally sensitive researcher in such circumstances would have proceeded somewhat differently, but also to good effect.

Sofia, who moved to New York without papers when she was nineteen, described herself as "well connected" [*bien conectada*]. She explained, in Spanish, "When I need something, I know I can turn to other people from my hometown. I got my cleaning job from my cousin, who told her boss about me. I got my daughter into the Head Start because my sister knew the director. I got free tickets to a movie the other day because my friend won them in a raffle. I always find a way." Sofia can be described as embedded in a rich resource network.

Here, the research did not begin with the concept of a "support network." The idea of the network came from Sofia. She described many different kinds of experiences. After some reflection and brainstorming, the researcher concluded that the idea of a "rich resource network" seemed to capture it well. Again, the reader can see directly that the author is offering a simplifying concept and can assess whether we believe that simplification was fair.

Finally, whether the researcher has worked deductively or inductively, how much they do with the resulting theoretical concept depends on the project, particularly whether it is primarily descriptive or explanatory. The preceding illustrations present researchers who mainly want to describe Sofia's network. Descriptive projects of this kind are among the most scientifically valuable pieces of qualitative scholarship, particularly when not much is known about the target population. For other projects, it is important to explain how the unraveled heterogeneity has come about. Such projects require the investigator to take further both kinds of tasks we have illustrated: to ask follow-up questions about the uncovered heterogeneity (e.g., "Why is it not appropriate to talk to them about personal things?") and to consider if and how to tie the resulting answers to a generalizing or simplifying concept. For still a third kind of project, it is important to explain the consequences, not causes, of the heterogeneity the research has uncovered. Such projects require an analogous process of asking follow-up questions and considering how to theorize.

The Group

Many in-depth interview studies focus not on individuals but on groups, classes, or other collectivities. Like the former kind, group-focused studies have often aimed to describe some aspect of their subjects' understanding, experiences, or motivations. In the discussion that follows, we neither repeat our discussion of each nor revisit our arguments about the importance of thoughtfulness when tying empirical heterogeneity to theoretical concepts, because regardless of whether the unit of analysis is the individual or the group, the overall points are the same.

Instead, we focus on the most distinct issue that arises when reporting heterogeneity in a group, which is how to deal with aggregation. When interviewers study groups, classes, or other collectivities, they ultimately want to aggregate observations from many individuals. Any such aggregation must reduce the actual complexity, and diversity, of the empirical world. However, effective researchers still tend to explicitly depict heterogeneity among groups, typically in one of two ways: by identifying exceptions to the aggregated pattern or by making heterogeneity itself the core characteristic depicted of the group. We discuss each in turn.

DEPICTING HETEROGENEITY AS EXCEPTION TO A GROUP PATTERN. For the sake of simplicity, our illustration assumes a study concerned with capturing perception (not experience or motivations) in a group. Suppose that, instead of having an interest in Sofia, the researcher is interested in describing how a large number of undocumented immigrants perceive their support networks. Consider the following passage:

> Mexican immigrants in New York are embedded in a network of support that provides information about jobs, help during emergencies, and emotional support. Sofia explained, in Spanish, "When I need something, I know I can turn to other people from my hometown." Patricio said something similar: "I was lucky to have friends that helped me when I lost my apartment." Miguel said, "I made it because I have a network that supports me."

This passage is perfectly reasonable. It provides evidence for its claim. Moreover, it offers evidence that more than one person reported this finding. The passage alone is no reason for concern with respect to heterogeneity. Yet if a manuscript on support networks in this group contained passage after passage of this kind—in which every interviewee quoted consistently offered evidence of the generalizing statement—then the reader would have reason to be suspicious. Either the author did not probe difference, or they did and decided to mask it.

A more effective researcher would, at a minimum, represent those who said something different. For example:

> Mexican immigrants in New York are embedded in a network of support that provides information about jobs, help during emergencies, and emotional support. Sofia explained, in Spanish, "When I need something, I know I can turn to other people from my hometown." Patricio said something similar: "I was lucky to have friends that helped me when I lost my apartment." But there were exceptions. Xiomara said, "I am mostly on my own here. Not many people to help me."

This statement is much more believable, because unless the researcher interviewed very few people, not finding such heterogeneity at all is unlikely. Note that we still must believe the author that Xiomara was an exception, while Sofia and Patricia were "the rule." However, an author who consistently reveals heterogeneity in contexts where we might expect it convinces us that that they sought it, and if they did then they clearly were inclined to probe the data as needed.

DEPICTING HETEROGENEITY AS CHARACTERISTIC OF THE GROUP. It is also possible that, for the particular issue of interest, there was no primary pattern to report, that instead, the core finding was heterogeneity. An entirely different strategy is to simply depict that heterogeneity.

Mexican immigrants in New York are embedded in diverse networks they sometimes perceive to be supportive but sometimes not. For example, Sofia explained, in Spanish, "When I need something, I know I can turn to other people from my hometown." But Isabela reported a different experience: "I am on my own here. My family—they have their own problems, and they cannot really help me." Juanita was ambivalent. "The family? They help sometimes, but sometimes they make you beg. It's not worth it. I can't wait until I don't have to ask them for help because they're always complaining."

This picture is, again, more persuasive than the one with which we started, because rather than masking the heterogeneity we know to exist, the researcher has bothered to make sense of it. This passage was largely about how participants understood their circumstances. A researcher interested in experience, motivation, or any other aspect of the people of interest may equally lean into, rather than ignore, the differences among participants in their study.

THE PROMISE AND PERIL OF REPORTING PERCENTAGES. Our discussion so far has featured illustrations in which findings were reported qualitatively, with no statistics or numbers whatsoever, because their focus has been how group members differ, not how many. But an entirely different approach, and one particularly tempting to those who hope their work will speak to quantitative researchers, is to report percentages. Because doing so can be thorny, it is worth some discussion.

Consider the author who uncovered some exceptions to the general pattern. The author may choose to report what they found as follows:

> Mexican immigrants in New York are embedded in a network of support that provides information about jobs, help during emergencies, and emotional support. As Sofia explained, in Spanish, "When I need something, I know I can turn to other people from my hometown." Among respondents, 56 percent reported that they were embedded in a network of support, 32 percent said that they were not, and the rest, 12 percent, were not clear one way or the other.

This strategy of reporting is borrowed directly from survey research. For interviewers with a large number of respondents, it can be an effective strategy, in that, in theory, it allows the reader to know exactly how much support there was for the generalizing statement. The reader can decide, on their own, whether 32 percent is significant enough a minority percentage to be concerned with.

However, reporting percentages can, in fact, constitute a *less accurate* way of reporting the data unless several important conditions are met. To see why, consider that accurately reporting the proportions of respondents who answered a question a given way requires every respondent to have received the same question, worded the same way, and in the same order. All three conditions matter. If not all respondents were asked the question, then we cannot know whether those who were not would have been sufficient to alter the observed distribution. If all respondents were asked the same question but it was worded differently in each case, then we cannot know whether they interpreted the different wordings similarly. For example, if one was asked "Do you have people who support you?" and another was asked "Can you count on your family?," we cannot be sure that any two affirmative answers are referring to the same thing.

And if all respondents were somehow asked the same question worded the same way but not in the same order, then everything that is known about how a question—and its answer—frames and changes how people interpret subsequent questions comes into play.[20] For example, people are typically more tired at the end of a long interview than at the beginning. As a result, if some of their early answers have usually led to follow-up questions, toward the end of the interview they might avoid those kinds of answers, to prevent extending the interview. Such effects have been documented multiple times and to dramatic effect.

But the importance of question order is not limited to fatigue. Whether in surveys or interviews, the conversation that preceded any given question will affect how the question is interpreted. If different people are asked questions in different orders, they may well report different answers, even when asked the same question.

Consider Miguel, who earlier reported that his network was the reason he "made it." Suppose the interviewer, before having met Miguel and interested in being able to report the percentage of respondents who had a support network, made sure to ask "Do you have a network that supports you?" worded precisely that way, in every interview. Over the course of a naturally flowing interview, an effective interviewer might have asked the question as follows:

INTERVIEWER: Have others you know had a difficult time?
MIGUEL: Yes, it's been tough. My older brother came to New York many years before me, and nothing worked out for him [*no le salió nada*] for a long time. He got a job in a restaurant but it didn't pay much. It was very difficult for him. He had no one until he sent for his wife. He didn't have the network.
INTERVIEWER: Do you have a network that supports you?
MIGUEL: I made it because I have a network that supports me.

That interview question and response is perfectly reasonable. But suppose the conversation had proceeded differently, as in-depth interviews often do.

INTERVIEWER: How did you meet Sofia?
MIGUEL: Well, she knows everyone. She knows people in the Head Start, the neighborhood, the church. I met her at church, but she knows everyone. She always talks about how connected she is but it's true. She has a big network.
INTERVIEWER: Do you have a network that supports you?
MIGUEL: Not that way, no.

Same question, different answer. When the interviewer follows the conversation where it goes, what survey researchers refer to as "question-order effects" will naturally follow. As we have said throughout this book, in in-depth interviewing, the researcher is not merely collecting but also producing the data.

For these reasons, any researcher willing to accurately describe a pattern with a precise percentage must conduct the interviews in ways that closely resemble surveys. In interview-based studies that are survey-like in nature, where the interviewer has a fixed protocol asked of every respondent, the needed conditions are more or less met, but only to the degree the interviewer is willing to limit follow-up questions and avoid a more natural conversation. Many in-depth interviewers are not willing to do so, for fear of undermining the very strengths of in-depth interviewing we have discussed so far. Some opt to just not report the percentage of respondents who answered open-ended questions in particular ways; others couple the interviews with separate surveys of the same respondents, reporting percentages from the survey data; and still others couple interviews with statistically representative surveys of the population at hand.[21]

In the end, as with everything we have discussed, the key to good work is a thoughtful approach to the collection and reporting of data.

An Example

In both individual- and group-focused studies, skilled interviewers have consistently produced narratives in which heterogeneity is central. An example is Cayce Hughes's study of the experiences of sixty-seven low-income African American mothers living in subsidized housing in the Sunnyside neighborhood of Houston.[22] Hughes found that mother after mother understood the institutional conditions of their home as living under official surveillance.

This common condition, however, manifested itself in diverse ways. For some, it was the constant video monitoring. As one of the interviewees, Jamilah, explained, "It's depressing. It's frustrating when you cannot—Your house do not even seem like your home no more, cause every time you walk out the door you looking at a damn camera.... What is the problem? What are you looking for? What are you looking for? ... It just feels like shit."[23] Jamilah was surprised to learn they were constantly video recorded. "Jamilah described coming home one day to find a violation notice on her apartment door, for 'littering and inappropriate conduct.' When Jamilah reported to the office to inquire, the property owner sat her down to watch video footage that appeared to show her toss a Coke can on the ground near the front gate."[24] Others, like Lonette, referred to an excess of trivial rules that could result in infractions and eviction. "We understand that you have a way you want us to live, but some of the rules ... they should not be there. I'm sorry. I just feel like a lot of things it is for him to keep us under control. He looking at us like a whole bunch of hoodlums out there sitting."[25] For still others, the jail-like random inspections were the issue: "Olivia described how, during random inspections, the property manager would 'bang on the door like she the police.... I didn't get a notice on my door or nothing.' She continued: 'She always say like little smart stuff like, "This is not your apartment, it's HUD's apartment, so whatever they rules are, you got to abide by them or you could be put out, you could be evicted." I'm like living over here sometimes with how she acts and how she talks to people, it's like being in prison.'"[26] Because we see clearly the diverse ways mothers experienced "living under surveillance," we know exactly the connection between empirical evidence and this concept, and we believe the author that it is an appropriate way to capture how the mothers understand their living situation.

Moreover, Hughes noted that in spite of this common understanding there was wide heterogeneity in responses to the surveillance mothers experienced. We cannot cover them in detail, but he showed that some mothers responded by staying inside as much as possible ("I do not even hardly go outside. . . . I'm in the house all the time"), others behaved as though they were cooperating, and others pushed back.[27] In all, the author presents such diversity of experiences and understandings that we trust his interpretations of events.

Heterogeneity in Participant Observation

As with interview-based research, when discussing how ethnographers can depict heterogeneity, it is useful to distinguish those focused on the individual from those focused on the group. But because ethnographers observe people in their contexts, they can also, instead, focus largely on the place. In what follows, we discuss each of the three in turn.

Because the primary means of data collection for the ethnographer is observation, any empirically detectable entity—anything a person can see, hear, smell, touch, or taste—is a potential source of data and a potential focus of study. Ethnographic studies thus range widely in both subject matter and approach, and an ethnographer can uncover heterogeneity in an essentially infinite number of ways. For example, an ethnographer focused just on individuals can study how they talk, dress, or carry themselves; how they interact with others; what experiences they have over the course of their days; how they interpret what they see; how they act upon expressed motives; who or what they avoid; and much more.

We cannot cover all. At the same time, we do not need to, because an illustration will suffice to demonstrate how describing heterogeneity in what is observed differs from doing so in what was elicited through an interview. Thus, for our discussion we assume that the researcher is interested in everyday experiences, as seen in the context of the individual, group, or place.

The Individual

Suppose, returning to Sofia and her networks, that the researcher is interested in the extent to which her everyday experiences suggest that she is well connected. After the fieldwork, the researcher reports the following:

> Sofia was embedded in a support network that provided information about jobs, help during emergencies, and emotional aid. At one of the community center's monthly meetings, Sofia was a few minutes late. In the meeting room, about a dozen women were seated around a table talking in pairs or groups of threes. She walked around the table, greeting everyone. She thanked one of them, her cousin Josefa, for the tip about the job. She thanked Yanina for the movie tickets, but laughed that her daughter slept her way through the film. The entire process took several minutes, after which she sat down, starting the meeting a few minutes late.

The passage is again perfectly reasonable. It makes a theoretical claim about Sofia and provides plenty of evidence for the claim. Furthermore, as we discuss in chapter 3, the evidence is concrete, lending credence to the idea that the author saw what is being reported. But if a scholarly work were based entirely on statements of this kind, all of them consistent with the claim that Sofia was well connected, then the reader would have cause to wonder whether the ethnographer did not observe carefully enough, or did so but took poor field notes, or took good field notes but did not examine them in depth, or examined them fully but chose to mask the diversity in the field. There are many ways that the heterogeneity observed in the field might be expressed. Two worth noting are heterogeneity in the recorded experience itself and heterogeneity across experiences.

DEPICTING HETEROGENEITY IN A GIVEN EXPERIENCE. The experience itself might have been more heterogeneous than described. Consider the following passage:

> Sofia was embedded . . . greeting everyone. She thanked one of them, her cousin Josefa, for the tip about the job. She thanked Yanina for the movie tickets, but laughed that her daughter slept her way through the film. After she mentioned the tickets, one pair of women glanced at each other and rolled their eyes. Sofia approached the others, but most of them nodded and returned to their conversations. The entire process took several minutes, after which she sat down, starting the meeting a few minutes late. Ana glared at Sofia, pointing repeatedly at her wristwatch.

The two passages could be describing the same experience. But because the researcher took care to report aspects of the recorded event that supported different ideas about the network, our impression of the circumstances, and of Sofia, is now different, more complex. We do not doubt that she is "embedded in a support network," but we know that it contains conflict as well as support.

DEPICTING HETEROGENEITY OF EXPERIENCES. Strong ethnographers often describe specific experiences or events when providing evidence of their claims. Reporting on different experiences that are diverse with respect to the topic at hand can deepen the reader's understanding of the circumstances and paint a picture that, by seeming more realistic, is more convincing.

Consider how a different ethnographer might have reported on Sofia's networks based on her everyday experiences.

> Sofia had attended two of the community center's monthly meetings. At the first, when she walked into the meeting room, about a dozen women were seated around a table talking in pairs or groups of threes. She walked around the table, greeting everyone. She thanked one of them, her cousin Josefa, for the tip about the job. She thanked Yanina for the movie tickets, but laughed that her daughter slept her way through the film. The entire process took several minutes, after which she sat down, starting the meeting a few minutes late. At the second meeting, the group was about the same size, but neither Sofia's cousin nor her friend Yanina was there. She looked around the room and nodded, and most of the women nodded in return. She sat silently, looking at her notes until start time.

The reader's view of the collective of experience is different. In the very first passage on the meetings, we had the impression that Sofia was an extrovert. Moreover, we inferred that her extroversion was probably the reason she had a strong network of support. Now we understand that her interactions with others may be conditional on whether she is already close to someone in the group. We also are not exactly sure how extensive her support network is.

We would need to see more, but we understand Sofia better and want to know more about her network.

The Group

Similar dynamics occur at the collective level. We need not belabor the points that we have made about groups, experiences, or observation. However, an example will make clear how important depicting either exceptions to a pattern or heterogeneity across people in a group can be.

Suppose that, instead of having an interest in Sofia, the researcher was interested in describing how a large number of undocumented immigrants like her understand themselves. Consider this passage:

> The women in the community center had formed a network of support that provided information about jobs, help during emergencies, and emotional support. Sofia had found her job through her cousin, who also participated in the meetings. Yanina had shared with others movie tickets she had won in a raffle. Claudia had babysat for Sofia, when the latter's daughter was too sick for day care.

By this point, the reader can surely imagine how different researchers might provide a more heterogeneous picture, depending on what the field-worker uncovered. As before, the researcher can paint the most common experience and identify exceptions or depict heterogeneity as a whole. For example:

> The women in the community center's monthly meetings had formed a network that sometimes proved supportive and sometimes

did not. Sofia had found her job through her cousin, who also participated in the meetings. Yanina had shared with others movie tickets she had won in a raffle. Ana, a group leader, seemed to nonetheless talk little to the others, and I never saw her ask anything of anyone—nor offer anything. In fact, many of the women did not linger after a meeting was over.

This and many variations on this theme would reveal the depths to which the researcher examined the work. The same is true in the representation of concepts, for which greater attention to heterogeneity is often a benefit.

The Place

Similarly important issues are at play when the ethnographer is interested in a place, such as an organization, a neighborhood, or a village, rather than in a person or set of persons. In such circumstances, attentiveness to heterogeneity can be particularly important, especially when describing contexts for which outgroup homogeneity bias is common, contexts such as low-income neighborhoods or rural towns.[28] To understand how, recall from chapter 1 our very first introduction to our hypothetical field-worker's report on Maria.

> Seventeen-year-old Maria lived in a predominantly black, high-poverty neighborhood in Philadelphia. She explained, "I don't like my neighborhood, and I can't wait to get out. My school counselor says that my grades are good enough to get me into Penn State, but I have to do well on the SAT to get a scholarship. I can't wait."

We have already discussed the potential problems with this passage with respect to cognitive empathy. But notice something else. Suppose that the research focus was not the person but the neighborhood. In that case, there would be two problems. First, the passage does not tell the reader much about the neighborhood. Second, the two facts the researcher does tell us about the neighborhood, that it is predominantly black and high poverty, seem to push the reader into an interpretation in which outgroup homogeneity bias is likely to play a role. Because of what we are told, we as readers fill in the blanks, and in such an exercise anything from stereotypes to prior books to film and television will likely play a role—we perceive it as crime-ridden or dirty or afflicted with high unemployment or underperforming schools.

Participant observers differ in what they look for and in what they have found. The researcher can have many interests regarding the place: who inhabits it, what it looks like, how it shapes behavior, how it has evolved, and more. In all such cases, the more exposure the ethnographer has had to the place, and the more time they have spent observing, taking careful field notes, and examining those field notes, the more heterogeneity they will naturally uncover. Conversely, if they do not report much heterogeneity around any of these dimensions, we have reason to question the reportage. Effective ethnographers are intuitively aware of this fact.

An Example

Consider Danielle Raudenbush's study of access to health care among low-income African Americans living in a housing development in a major US city.[29] The (pseudonymous) Jackson Homes development typifies extreme urban poverty at the start of the twenty-first century. As she explained, "Jackson Homes is highly segregated by race; more than 95 percent of its residents are African American. [The neighborhood in which it] is situated has a poverty rate of above 50 percent, which makes it what sociologists call an extreme poverty area."[30] In fact, the neighborhood's poverty and crime rates are each about three times higher than those of the city. "It is geographically isolated from areas of commerce and places of employment."[31] The nearest real grocery store "is a bus or car ride away, which presents challenges for residents who may not have access to transportation."[32] "It was built close to several active and inactive landfills, a sewage treatment plant, oil refineries, and many heavy manufacturing facilities. Several sites around the development . . . are classified as hazardous waste facilities."[33] The site is among the poorest, most segregated, most crime-ridden, most isolated, and most racially homogenous black neighborhoods in the country.

Not surprisingly, it also has what Raudenbush described as "elevated rates of many health problems. These include low-birth-weight infants, infant mortality, and lead poisoning. This area also has higher rates of death by many diseases [than the rest of the] city, including death from chronic respiratory disease, coronary heart disease, stroke, diabetes-related death, and homicide."[34] Life expectancy is six years lower than the city average.

Given how little is known about access to health care in such conditions, anything Raudenbush uncovered about how this population gains access to health care would be informative. With close to thirty million Americans still uninsured, many of the people in the country most disadvantaged with respect to health care are surely among her respondents. In such circumstances, depicting a homogenous picture that explains the primary way health-care access is difficult might seem to be expected and even justifiable, since such extreme conditions likely affect everyone and, in any case, any differences within, one might think, pale in comparison to differences to those in the outside world. Yet Raudenbush, an empirically careful ethnographer, did not observe homogeneity:

> There is considerable variation in the extent to which my participants are able to access health services. While they are all low-income African Americans that reside within a single neighborhood, they are not monolithic in their experiences of poverty. [For example, residents] vary in their insurance status . . . although even among those that have insurance, some face obstacles to care. Additionally, despite all being classified as very low-income, they differ in income levels and the amount of cash they have on hand, which in turn affects their ability to obtain various aspects of care. These include, for example, being able to pay for co-payments or transportation to and from health care appointments. People also differ in terms of whether they legally reside in the housing development, which can affect their ability to get care.[35]

Indeed, as Raudenbush explains, "Some residents see doctors regularly and do not have difficulty obtaining needed care. Others, though, face obstacles to care and are unable to access health services, even when they are very sick."[36] The chapter went on to describe this heterogeneity in great detail, comparing the experiences of residents like Cassandra, who, on both food stamps and Supplemental Security Income and making ends meet with babysitting, janitorial, and other work, is both Medicare and Medicaid eligible and thus "highly integrated into the healthcare system" to those of individuals like Diana, who, on food stamps but without SSI, other cash assistance, regular work, much furniture, or custody of her children, is thus without Medicaid or regular access to formal health care.[37]

In addition to describing these differences, Raudenbush explained the consequences extensively. Though we cannot do the book justice in these pages, one issue makes clear how probing heterogeneity allows a skilled ethnographer to understand her site much more effectively. Consider that Raudenbush's ultimate finding was that health care in areas such as Jackson Homes was essentially a "hybrid" of formal and informal elements, as people used whatever means they could to access needed medication or care. It turns out that "heterogeneity in access to care among residents [was] central to the hybrid health care system. In Jackson Homes some people have access to health services and are thus able to obtain health-related resources like medication and medical equipment, while others do not have access to health services. This heterogeneity means that there is a demand for medication and medical equipment from people who do not have access to health services, as well as a supply of these resources from the people who do have access to health services."[38] The resulting analysis, a combination of careful observation and thoughtful theorizing, is the mark of an effective ethnography.

Conclusion

We have discussed and presented many forms of heterogeneity. Our point is not that any good project must depict all of them; in fact, most projects cannot, and further, a project may display forms of heterogeneity beyond those captured here. Instead, our point is that an article or book that depicts none of them is deeply suspect. And these do occur. For example, in the interest of speaking to policy on an important social problem, some researchers ignore the heterogeneity in their data and instead present mainly evidence consistent with a bottom-line story. Others, hoping to offer a memorable theory or idea, exclude cases that do not fit a central point. Still others, in an effort to meet journal word limits, ignore heterogeneity rather than narrowing their research question. Most of these strategies undermine, rather than strengthen, the empirical grounding of a qualitative study. The qualitative researcher's most important asset is proximity to the world, and we know the world is diverse and messy. Good field-workers cannot help but uncover this diversity and to report what they have uncovered.

3 Palpability

Our discussions of cognitive empathy and heterogeneity have shown that these indicators of quality can be detected in a narrative's extended passages. Our third indicator, palpability, can be detected in as little as a single sentence, because it is a feature of every piece of evidence reported. Palpability, as we use the term, is the extent to which the reported findings are presented concretely rather than abstractly.

Most of the passages we have presented as illustrations of high cognitive empathy and heterogeneity also demonstrated palpable reporting. For this reason, this chapter is brief, focusing on exactly what gives palpable evidence its character. The chapter shows that even concise discussions that aim to neither demonstrate empathy nor reveal heterogeneity can differ dramatically in quality, by virtue of how concrete the evidence reported is.

Background

Concreteness

Though the term "palpable" is rarely found in qualitative textbooks, it is implicit in what they encourage budding researchers to aim for. It is also a consistent characteristic of the evidence that strong qualitative studies produce. Palpable evidence is concrete. To understand concreteness, consider its opposite, abstraction. For a researcher to identify any pattern in the data, they must perform an abstraction: they must decide that two direct observations—two statements uttered by interviewees, two actions noticed in the field, and so forth—are versions of a general phenomenon, even an only slightly more general phenomenon. For example, a researcher interviewing mothers must decide that when one interviewee says, "My husband and I argued" and another says "Jeff was being annoying," they are both expressing the general phenomenon, *spousal conflict*, rather than, say, one expressing that the couple argued and the other that the spouse was joking. Over the course of a study, small abstractions of this kind become larger and more encompassing abstractions that result in a scientific contribution. Abstraction of one or another form is the foundation of social science, the feature that converts a single observation into a principle, theory, or hypothesis.[1]

But abstractions are not, in fact, data, and a study of any kind that reports only abstractions, even highly specific abstractions, is presenting an interpretation of the data, not the data themselves.[2] The qualitative data themselves, as we have said, are the statements elicited during a particular interview and the observations recorded at a specific time in a given space. Thus, only quotations and field reports have a chance of constituting palpable evidence.

But quotations and field notes are not necessarily enough; closeness matters, too. By closeness we refer to proximity to the phenomenon of interest, and field-workers can fail to get close when collecting data. Interviewers can elicit quotations that are themselves abstractions or generalizations of the phenomenon;

ethnographers can fail to either observe or record the phenomenon of interest closely. In either case, a clue that the researcher failed to get close is their reliance on generalizations in the quotations or field notes.

Rather than being general, palpable evidence is particular. When strong interview studies make a claim about participants' perceptions, meanings, or motivations, they quote particular people who perceived and assigned meaning to specific things, and they report the motives the people expressed behind distinct actions undertaken. When strong ethnographies make a claim about conditions in a neighborhood, organization, or other setting, they introduce specific events, places, situations, and interactions, rather than just asserting there was a pattern; they report actions that happened in a particular place at a particular time. Ultimately, only reports of distinct persons, statements, perceptions, meanings, motivations, events, actions, responses, and places have a chance of constituting palpable evidence.[3]

Palpable Statements

Consider how a single empirical statement might exhibit palpability. While a single statement is rarely enough to report findings, beginning here will make everything else about palpability clearer. Imagine an interview-based study of how mothers manage conflicts with husbands around keeping children safe from harm. Suppose the study asserted the following: "Mothers reported being more concerned about their children's safety than their spouses are." While the statement is perfectly clear, it lacks palpable evidence. It certainly reports *on* data, but does not actually provide the data.

As a solution, one approach might be to quantify the report. For example: "Mothers reported being more concerned about their children's safety than their spouses are: seventeen of twenty mothers described themselves as more concerned; one described the father as more concerned; the rest described both as equally concerned." That statement is more detailed than the original, because it contains quantitative data. However, it does not actually report more palpable qualitative evidence. With respect to the latter, it is equally unpalpable.

A second approach might be to add a quote: "Mothers reported being more concerned about their children's safety than their spouses are. As one of them explained, 'I tend to worry a lot more than he does.'" This statement does present qualitative evidence. We can see directly that at least one mother believes she worries more than her spouse. However, the statement from the mother is itself a generalization, a summary of the specific interactions with her husband from which she has collectively drawn the inference that she "tends to worry a lot more." Since all we have is her summary, we do not have evidence for the basis of her perception. The evidence presented has limited palpability and is therefore relatively weak.

A third approach adds a quote that gets closer, as we have used the term, to the phenomenon at hand: "Mothers reported being more concerned about their children's safety than their spouses are. As one of them explained, 'The last time we got in the car, I wouldn't leave until everyone was fully buckled, and he complained that we were only driving a few blocks. I worry more than he does.'" Because the mother reported a particular event with a particular response, we understand far more clearly the source of her generalization. The qualitative evidence is much stronger.

When its evidence is palpable, a study reports far more details about events, situations, people, and places, and therefore comes across as richer. But richness itself is not necessarily a sign of quality, because details may not be palpable (as when they are largely about participants' generalizations), may not be offered in service of an empirical statement (as when they just add color), or may not relate to the qualitative data (as when they merely quantify how many people reported something). Palpable evidence produces rich narratives, but narratives that seem rich may actually lack palpability.

We discuss the form that palpable evidence takes in in-depth interview and in participant observation research.[4]

Palpability in In-Depth Interviewing

To produce palpable interview data, quoting participants directly is necessary. But it is no guarantee, because the quotations themselves may be unpalpable, if they failed to get close to an interviewee's base perceptions, beliefs and attitudes, interpretations, motives, or experiences. Getting close requires specificity, which will often need to be elicited.

It is common among budding interviewers to ask questions that elicit from participants only broad generalizations about their lives. This practice may stem from the belief that social science should aim for generalizations, such that aspects of people's lives that appear unique should not be the focus of study. (The practice may also be a misapplication of the formal idea by King, Keohane, and Verba that there are systematic and nonsystematic components to every particular case.)[5] For example, an inexperienced interviewer interested in marital conflict might be inclined to ask a participant, "Do you tend to fight often with your partner" rather than ask "Can you tell me about the last fight you had?" Informed by training in basic statistics, they might fear that the last fight, or any single fight, is not representative of the true experience, opting instead to ask the more general question, presumably to get at the underlying true pattern.

Asking people to report on a general trend or pattern in their lives is often necessary, and the practice is in fact common in survey research. The problem with relying on this approach for an in-depth interview study is neither that generalizations are not important (they are necessary) nor that a particular event is not unique (it could be). The problem is that an interview consisting primarily of questions of this kind will yield little useful qualitative data, because the responses by the interviewee will already be one step abstracted from experience. The interviewee will essentially report their own generalizations, which means that the interviewer can do little more than report abstractions from another person's abstractions. The interview will defeat the purpose of qualitative interviewing, and the final report, if based largely on interviews of that kind, will be unconvincing.[6]

A study can only report palpable statements when the interviewer took care to elicit them. While the techniques for doing so are best left to handbooks, a brief illustration is useful.[7] In the study of mothers and children's safety, the researcher who failed to elicit palpable data might have conducted an interview as follows:

INTERVIEWER: How much do you worry about the safety of your child?

GINA: A lot. I'm her mother. It's my job to. Especially because she's not old enough yet to know what's safe and what isn't. So, I have to keep an eye on her all the time.

INTERVIEWER: And what about your partner? How important is safety to him?

GINA: [*Laughs*] I mean, of course he thinks her safety is important. But we have some . . . [*pauses*] different ideas about what's actually safe.

INTERVIEWER: Who do you think is more concerned about your child's safety—you or your partner?

GINA: Me, definitely. I tend to worry a lot more than he does.

The problem here is that on the core matter at hand, understanding Gina's worry, the interviewer only asked Gina to generalize from experience (e.g., "How much do you worry?," "Who worries more?"). To be sure, the interviewer did several things well, including asking clear questions, allowing Gina to think before concluding one of her answers, and explicitly asking Gina to compare herself to her husband. But on the basis of this interview, the researcher would not have been able to produce more qualitative evidence about the mother's greater concern than, "As one of them explained, 'I tend to worry a lot more than he does.'" They simply would not have the data.

To produce better data, the researcher could have approached the interview in at least two different ways. One approach, based on questions planned in advance, is generally deductive; the other, based on responses to the participant in the interview, is more inductive. The approaches result in somewhat different data, but in both cases the resulting evidence is more palpable.

Planned

Interviewers who approach their work deductively carefully design their questionnaires in advance. For the hypothetical study at hand, an experienced researcher would ensure the core question asks the participant not to report on their general trend or practice but on a specific event, situation, phenomenon, or practice. Rather than "How much do you worry about the safety of your child?," they might prepare one of the following as the core question: "Can you tell me about a time when you and your partner had different ideas about your child's safety?," or "Do you and your partner agree on whether children should wear masks during COVID-19?," or "Some people say that, compared to when we were children, parents today worry too much about children's physical safety, not letting them roam, fall, and get small cuts and bruises. Do you agree? Does your partner?" These questions differ in topic and approach. Nonetheless, by focusing on the particular, all provide the space for more palpable evidence.

In practice, interviewers who approach their work deductively tend to prepare follow-up questions after each core question (an issue we discuss at length in chapter 4). The resulting interview might proceed as follows:

INTERVIEWER: Can you tell me about a time when you and your partner had different ideas about your daughter's safety?
GINA: Oh my god, it's constant. Like, yesterday, I asked Matthew to watch her because I had to go to the bathroom. And she's just starting to crawl now, and I was freaking out, because when I came out, she had crawled over—she's never gotten that far before! And she was reaching for the TV wires, and I was scared to death that she might pull them and the whole TV would come crashing down on her.
INTERVIEWER: What did you do?

GINA: I ran over and I scooped her up and I was just holding her and telling her that the wires aren't safe and that I was so glad she was okay. And, I mean, it's kind of embarrassing, but I just started sobbing. Just holding her and crying right there in the living room.

INTERVIEWER: What was Matthew doing?

GINA: [*Laughs*] Yeah, he was actually, like, six feet away the whole time—sitting on the couch, doing god-knows-what on his phone. He didn't even notice that she was reaching for the wires. Totally oblivious. So, I had to run right past him and grab her and pull her away. And I probably yelled at him for not watching her closely enough. I think I told him I can't trust him.

INTERVIEWER: What did he say?

GINA: He just kept saying: "It's fine. She's fine. It's okay."

The data produced are inevitably much more concrete; the resulting evidence, much more palpable.

Unplanned

The interviewer may not have begun the study with an interest in understanding couples' disagreements about children's safety. Instead, the idea may have emerged over the course of an interview about, say, parenting. In that situation, the interviewer cannot plan in advance to ask questions about specific moments of safety-related conflict in participants' lives. Instead, the interviewer must notice safety as an emerging theme in a participant's responses and ask follow-up questions that call for concrete examples that illustrate that theme. Consider an example.

INTERVIEWER: Do you and your partner ever have different ideas about parenting?

GINA: We're mostly on the same page, but when it comes to safety stuff, I'm more neurotic, and Matthew is more laid back.

INTERVIEWER: What do you mean?

GINA: Obviously, Matthew cares about Aisha's safety. But he doesn't notice things the way I do. That's why I haven't left them alone together yet. I mean, I'm guessing nothing terrible would happen, but you never know.

INTERVIEWER: You said Matthew doesn't always notice things. Can you give me an example?

GINA: Like, Matthew didn't grow up around kids like I did. He was the youngest, and he wasn't babysitting cousins or anything like that. He'd never even changed a diaper before Aisha was born. And even now, when he does change her, I end up having to fix it, because it's not fastened right, or it's crooked or whatever, and if I don't fix it, it ends up leaking all over the place. Then I have to clean up the mess. So, I just wish Matthew would notice things more—notice when the diaper isn't fastened right, or notice that the car seat buckle is in the wrong place, or that the outlet cover didn't get put back in.

Though the interviewer began with parenting disagreements in general, Gina brought up safety. But she only offered a generalization: "Matthew is a lot more laid back." Even when pressed for more detail, she again responded with a generalization: "Matthew doesn't always notice things." Rather than stop, the interviewer asked explicitly for an example, resulting in more concrete data. (See also chapter 4.)

An Example

Effective interview-based studies almost always report palpable evidence. Consider Jennifer Lee and Min Zhou's book *The Asian American Achievement Paradox*, which is based on life history interviews in Los Angeles with children of immigrants from China, Vietnam, and Mexico; people who were born in those countries and emigrated as children; and others.[8] The authors argue that the idea of "a good education" means different things to different people. As they explain:

> Some groups frame a good education as graduating from high school, attending a local community college, and earning an occupational certificate that allows them to work as electricians, mechanics, or nursing or dental assistants. Others adopt a much narrower frame that involves getting straight A's and graduating as the high school valedictorian, gaining admission to an elite university, and earning a graduate degree in medicine, law, science, or engineering. Hence, groups may value education equally, but they may construct remarkably different frames of what a 'good' education is and what success means.[9]

Their evidence derives from interviews. While space constraints prevent a full accounting of the evidence they provide, an example will suffice to make the point that effective interviewers can elicit palpable evidence about an abstract idea such as "a good education." Consider a passage containing a quote from Caroline, a thirty-five-year-old woman whose parents were born in China. We learn from Caroline that her family's particular understanding of a good education involved attaining an advanced degree. And from Caroline we obtain palpable evidence about how she sees this understanding:

> The idea of graduating from high school for my mother was not a great, congratulatory day. I was happy, but you know what? My mother was very blunt, she said, "This is a good day, but it's not that special." She finds it absurd that graduating from high school is made into a big deal because you should graduate high school; everyone should. It's not necessarily a privilege; it's an obligation. You must go to high school, and you must finish. It's a further obligation that you go to college and get a bachelor's degree. Thereafter, if you get a PhD or a master's, that's the big thing; that's the icing on the cake with a cherry on top, and that's what she values.[10]

The reader gets a clear understanding of how Caroline views her mother's understanding of a good education: it is that which surpasses the basic obligation of high school and college.

Palpability in Participant Observation

In any social setting, the number of details an ethnographer could record is infinite. An interaction as innocuous as the purchase of a cup of coffee by a customer at a café involves a vast number of elements regarding the people and their actions, including the color of each person's clothes, hair, and eyes; the tenor of their voice; every utterance they make; every movement of their body; and every reaction to each action, gesture, or inaction. What the ethnographer could record includes every aspect of the setting, including the smell of the coffee shop; the peaks and dips of the background noise; the jingle of the doorbell; the brightness, hue, and position of the lights; the clustering of seats; the hardness of the floors, tables, and chairs; and the chill of air. An ethnographer who tried to capture everything would never finish taking field notes. But one who ignored details in favor of issues that presumably seemed important would be destined to discover little they did not already know or believe and would also, inevitably, produce weak data.

Consider a study of gender and parenting in which the researcher observes couples with young children. The study centers on a few couples who are shadowed for months as they go about their lives. The study might report the disagreement and offer a case as evidence.

> The couples I observed disagreed at least occasionally about children's safety, and when they did, mothers displayed more concern than fathers did. For example, Isabel and Akio often argued about issues such as car seats, with Isabel taking the more careful stance.

The passage generalizes the experience of Isabel and Akio and lacks palpability.

Improving the palpability of the evidence would require, as we have said, focusing on the particular. There are as many ways of doing so as there are elements of an interaction or site that an ethnographer could observe. But we can illustrate the point by focusing on two common practices, centering on particular events and particular people.

Reporting on Events

One way a researcher comes to understand a condition or predicament as such—for example, to understand a couple as disagreeing over safety—is by conceptually aggregating multiple events in which the predicament manifested itself. Knowing that the aggregation itself does not constitute data, effective ethnographers often center on particular events to provide palpable evidence. Indeed, a frequent focus on distinct events is a common sign of a skilled ethnographer. Thus, an improved version of the preceding passage could depict a particular event:

> The couples I observed disagreed at least occasionally about children's safety, and when they did, mothers displayed more concern than fathers did. For example, on a short drive to meet friends for dinner, Isabel and Akio argued over whether to adjust the straps on their toddler Ren's car seat. Isabel wanted to remove the car seat and adjust the straps to better fit Ren, but Akio resisted, saying that Ren would be fine. Ultimately, they decided not to adjust the straps after Akio agreed to adjust them later.

The evidence is clearly more palpable. The researcher has reported on a distinct event that makes clear exactly how disagreements unfolded.

The researcher may also increase the palpability of the description by telling us exactly what the participants in the event have said.

> The couples I observed disagreed at least occasionally about children's safety, and when they did, mothers displayed more concern than fathers did. For example, before a short drive to meet friends for dinner, Isabel told Akio, "The straps are too low. We have to remove the car seat to fix them."
>
> "We don't have time, honey," said Akio. Isabel replied: "What's more important, 10 minutes or your child's safety?"

"You always do this!"

Ultimately, they decided not to adjust the straps after Akio agreed to adjust them later.

Because we directly access what the participants said, we understand them better. Thus, we better understand the nature of the disagreements. Whether to offer quotations will depend on the aims of the study and whether the researcher, given the context in which fieldwork was conducted, would have been in a position to record those accurately. If they are reliably available, they can provide powerful palpable evidence.

If the disagreements over safety are not central to the study, then either of the passages might be sufficient. If they are central, then understanding the perceptions, meanings, or motivations underlying disagreements would likely be important. If so, the ethnographer might offer a more palpable account of the situation. The researcher could do so even if they were not in a position to record exact quotations.

The couples I observed disagreed at least occasionally about children's safety, and when they did, mothers displayed more concern than fathers did, often conceiving of the same problems differently. For example, on a short drive to meet friends for dinner, Isabel and Akio argued over whether to adjust the straps on their toddler Ren's car seat. Isabel, sitting on the front passenger seat, watched as Akio buckled Ren into the car. This was their first car ride in weeks, and Ren had recently experienced a growth spurt. Isabel told Akio that Ren's shoulders were now too high on the straps, per the manual's instructions. She asked that they remove the car seat, adjust the position of the straps, and put it back together to improve Ren's safety. Akio dismissed the concern, noting that they would be late for dinner, that the drive was only a few miles, and that Ren would be fine. Ultimately, they decided not to adjust the straps after Akio agreed to adjust them later.

Here, the ethnographer offered much more evidence to understand the event. We learn that Ren had experienced a growth spurt, that they had not driven in several weeks, and that Isabel had read the manual. The situation comes across in clearer relief, and we better understand the larger points—that parents disagreed over safety and that they conceived the same problems differently. If quoting Akio and Ren directly were possible, then adding their voices would strengthen the evidentiary basis of the passage even further.

Reporting on People

An entirely different way of increasing the palpability of an account is by providing more concrete data on the people involved. This approach may be valuable if a study is less concerned with predicaments than with people. For example, rather than adding palpable evidence about a situation, the researcher may add it about the persons involved.

> The couples I observed disagreed at least occasionally about children's safety, and when they did, mothers displayed more concern than fathers did. For example, Isabel and Akio approached their toddler Ren's safety differently: Isabel had carefully reviewed studies over the proper age at which to switch Ren to a forward-facing seat, ordered allergen tests when Ren appeared to break out

slightly once after eating yogurt, and insisted on buying a child-proof guard for their living room fireplace. On each of these issues, Akio had said she was overthinking things.

This passage does not give us details on any particular event. But it tells us a lot about Isabel and Akio by describing multiple concrete aspects of their personality, with Isabel coming across as more careful than Akio. We understand with far greater clarity than when we had only heard, "Isabel and Akio often argued about issues such as car seats, with Isabel taking the more careful stance."

Depending on the context, the researcher may also combine palpable descriptions of events and people. For example:

Isabel, sitting on the front passenger seat, watched as Akio buckled Ren into the car. This was their first car ride in weeks, and Ren had recently experienced a growth spurt.

"The straps are too low," she said. "Ren's bigger. I remember reading in the manual that at this point we have to remove the car seat and readjust them."

Isabel had spent weeks studying everything about car seats, including the right position of the shoulder straps and the proper age at which to switch to forward-facing seats.

"You're always doing this!" said Akio.

The narrative would naturally be much longer. Whether doing this is the right strategy would depend, again, on the point of the study. In this respect, the effective ethnographer would have exercised as much judiciousness about how much palpable evidence to report as the effective survey analysis would have about how many tables to produce.

An Example

An example of effectively palpable reporting can be found in Barrie Thorne's classic analysis of how girls and boys play based on ethnographic observation in two elementary schools.[11] Thorne argues that, through many rituals, children enforce symbolic boundaries between boys and girls.

While some of the rituals are practiced equally by girls and boys, others are practiced mainly by boys, who use them to assert themselves over the girls. Thorne explains: "On the playgrounds of both schools I repeatedly saw boys, individually or in groups, deliberately disrupt the activities of groups of girls. Boys ruin ongoing games of jump rope by dashing under the twirling rope and disrupting the flow of the jumpers or by sticking a foot into the rope and stopping its momentum."[12] Notice that in the passage, Thorne describes exactly what kind of ritual she observed.

However, the statements themselves are generalizations of her observations, rather than strictly palpable evidence. A skilled ethnographer, Thorne then provides the latter, using the technique of describing a concrete event.

On the Ashton playground seven fourth-grade girls engaged in an intense game of four-square. It was a warm October day, and the girls had piled their coats on the cement next to the painted court. Two boys, mischief enlivening their faces, came to the edge of the court. One swung his arm into the game's bouncing space; in annoyed response, one of the female players pushed back at him. He ran off for a few feet, while the other boy circled in to take a swipe, trying to knock the ball out of play. Meanwhile, the first boy kneeled behind the pile of coats and leaned around to watch the girls. One of the girls yelled angrily, "Get out. My glasses are in one of those, and I don't want 'em busted." A playground aide called the boys over and told them to "leave the girls alone," and the boys ran off.[13]

Thorne offers a concrete depiction of an actual event that took place, getting herself, and the reader, close to the phenomenon at hand. She describes the warmth of the day; the coats on the black-top; the four-square game being played; and the number, ages, and genders of the people involved. She also describes how the inter-action between those people unfolded—for example, that the girls are playing "intensely." Readers know exactly what she observed and can make our own inferences about how it relates to the gen-eral proposition.

Conclusion

Our discussion should have made clear that, when interviewers and ethnographers get close to the phenomena at hand, they collect far more data than a manuscript can report on. To the untrained eye, lengthy interview quotes and detailed descriptions might seem like window dressing, unnecessary flourishes added merely to in-crease the reader's engagement with or enjoyment of the text. And in unskilled hands they can be, as when they are not in service of an empirical proposition or when the quotes or observations are them-selves abstractions. But as we have shown, palpable evidence does not necessarily derive from detail, or length, or richness as such; it results from concrete data that got close to the phenomenon at hand by centering on particular events, persons, utterances, inter-actions, or other pieces of elicited or observed data. Palpability in evidence is the foundation of an empirically convincing text.

4 Follow-Up

We define follow-up as the extent to which the researcher collected data to answer questions that arose during the data-collection process itself. Our discussions of cognitive empathy, heterogeneity, and palpability illustrated several times how interviewers improved the quality of the data by following up on participants' statements. Those points need not be repeated. But following up is not just a feature of interviews; it plays a role in ethnographies as well, and it in fact can describe an orientation to the entire data-collection process, representing a foundation of true scientific discovery. This chapter clarifies why follow-up matters, presents several different forms it can take, and shows how it can be detected in the finished manuscript.

Background

Qualitative data always constitute what sociologists would term an "emergent entity," one that cannot strictly be forecast because it is the product of an interaction. The data result not from the actions of one party but from the interactions between them.[1] In those interactions, the real-time decisions of both participants and researchers matter. As we discussed in the introduction, what the field-worker does when running interviews or collecting field notes might most accurately be described as not collecting but producing the data. Field-workers react in real time to the events before them, either asking or failing to ask questions in response to what was uttered, and either directing or not directing attention toward an event that happens before them. The researcher must decide, and such decisions affect the content and overall quality of the data.

Thus, it is impossible to determine in a strict sense the rules for researchers to follow in ensuring that the finished product has effectively followed up on emerging issues. The researchers could certainly have planned to ask about given topics or to focus on certain issues and could even have prepared responses or reactions to anticipated answers or events. But any such plans would have faced the reality of the field. The participants in every in-depth interview would have said different things; those at every field site, done different things. And every researcher would have responded to each statement or action differently. Indeed, in a telling collaborative study, Reuben May and Mary Pattillo-McCoy visited the same field site with the same objective at the same time, then wrote their field notes separately.[2] Their reactions to simultaneous events made clear how much difference the idiosyncrasies of the field-worker make in the nature of recorded data.

Nevertheless, there is a major difference in quality between interviews in which the researcher did not ask follow-up questions and those in which they did, as well as between field notes in which the observer did not follow up on leads and those in which they did. Moreover, although no researcher can follow up on every action or deed—and thus no two researchers will have followed up on exactly the same issues—for any given empirical claim a reader can certainly assess objectively whether the researcher followed up as needed about that claim. When the researcher fails to do so, the evidence for the claim will lack depth and palpability. For claims about what people perceived, what it meant to them, or what motivated their actions, the narrative will often lack cognitive empathy. For claims about what they experienced, about their characteristics, or about conditions in a site, it will likely lack depth, heterogeneity, or both. Thus, we examine how effective follow-up can be detected in the finished product.

One clarification is important. In previous chapters, we have shown that field researchers sometimes approach their work deductively and sometimes inductively, and this difference in approach applies to following up. For example, an interviewer may prepare specific follow-up questions in advance or instead create them spontaneously during the session in response to new statements. The advantage of the former is that such questions ensure the researcher can examine theories or propositions they knew in advance that they wanted to test. The advantage of the latter is that such questions allow the researcher to discover new aspects of the phenomenon or people at hand that they had not thought about or considered. Still, a project that *only* followed up deductively would have done something different from what we are describing here. Certainly such a project would be much more likely to produce good data than one in which the researcher did not follow up at all, and previous chapters have shown illustrations of why that is the case. But the project would not actually be responsive to the new prompts emerging in the field, since the researcher would have only responded to those statements they had anticipated.

For this reason, experienced field-workers, even those who primarily work deductively, almost always follow up inductively: they respond to new statements or actions that emerge in an interview or observation by following the lead wherever it goes. This kind of inductive follow-up is what we refer to when we state that effective follow-up involves responsiveness to issues that arose in the field itself. And it is the focus of this chapter.

Follow-Up in In-Depth Interviewing

In theory, interviewers could follow up on statements from participants in an infinite number of ways. In practice, those strategies typically take one of five basic forms. Each inevitably produces better data, but they result in different kinds of findings. We discuss each in turn.

Five Approaches

NEW QUESTION. One particularly common strategy is to follow up on a participant's statement by asking an unplanned question. The decision to develop and ask a new question in the moment is fundamental; in fact, it is arguably the most important difference between an in-depth interview question and an open-ended question in a survey. Survey questionnaires, normally composed of fixed-answer, multiple-choice, or otherwise closed questions, often include open-ended questions that allow the respondent to answer freely. But in the context of a formal survey, the surveyor typically does not then ask a follow-up question they decided on the spot. In the context of an in-depth interview, the researcher generally expects to ask questions that were not previously planned.

Consider a study based on interviews with midlevel managers of nonprofit organizations about how they conceive of their work.[3] An interviewer who failed to follow up with new questions might proceed as follows:

INTERVIEWER: How would you describe the kind of work your organization does?

KEITH: My boss likes to say we're all about CSR. [*Scoffs.*] But really, we do client management.

INTERVIEWER: And how would you describe your role in the organization?

KEITH: A little bit of everything: writing proposals, meeting with the corporate bigwigs, putting together budgets and reports. I'd love to spend more time actually working on real projects, but lately it's more behind-the-scenes stuff.

The interviewer moved quickly from one prepared question to the next without asking Keith to elaborate. In doing so, the interviewer failed to clarify the meaning of jargon ("CSR," "client management"). They also failed to follow up on Keith's "bread crumbs," allusions to ideas, events, or people that were not directly asked about but that, at least from the perspective of the respondent, are potentially relevant to the point they are trying to convey. Bread crumbs often point to difficult or sensitive parts of the respondent's life, and they can sometimes be identified by respondents' emotionally loaded actions (e.g., tears, laughter), tones (e.g., sarcasm, excitement), or words. Bread crumbs are essentially either deliberate or unwitting invitations to the interviewer to follow up.

For example, Keith scoffed, which was an indication about what he thought about either his boss or his boss's statement.

Rather than following up, the interviewer continued, either because they had a set script, were not paying sufficient attention, or were only concerned with a narrow set of issues, or for some other reason. Regardless of the reason, not asking Keith to clarify left the reader uncertain as to what Keith meant. Instead, the interviewer could have followed up with an unplanned question in several different ways: "What is CSR?," or "Why do you think it's really client management, instead of CSR?," or "Why do you think your boss calls it CSR?" Any of these would have produced deeper data about the kind of work the organization does. We have seen several illustrations throughout the book.

NEW INTERVIEW. A second approach is following up with a new interview. Follow-up interviews may be planned in advance or may be responses to unfinished conversations, and their role in the completed manuscript will depend in part on how they emerged. But they remain a powerful way to address in-depth issues that emerged in an interview, regardless of whether they did not arise in the former because a second one was anticipated, there was too much to cover, the researcher forgot, or the researcher, having started to analyze the data, realized a follow-up would be important.

Consider Keith's case. The significance of his scoff may not have become clear until the end of the interview, the point at which the researcher realized that Keith had scoffed at every mention of his boss or at every mention of the idea of "CSR" or of "corporate social responsibility." Returning to the issue in a second interview would allow the researcher to collect the data needed to understand it, should it prove important to a claim. The resulting narrative about Keith and his relations to his boss would be far more accurate, with greater depth.

NEW PARTICIPANT. A third approach is following up with a new participant. Researchers differ in whether they approach sample selection more deductively or more inductively.[4] They also differ in the extent to which they vary questions across respondents. But all effective researchers see new issues arise before they have interviewed all participants, and given the unpredictability of open-ended in-depth interviews, all such interviews inevitably vary from participant to participant. Suppose again that Keith, one of the first participants interviewed, had scoffed or expressed disapproval at every mention of CSR. If reinterviewing Keith were not part of the design (in a strictly deductive model), not practically feasible (because he had transferred overseas), or not ethically possible (because he formally declined to be recontacted), then following up with other respondents may be an alternative.

But turning to others is not only useful as a "plan B." At the end of Keith's interview, an attentive interviewer may wonder if Keith's disapproval of CSR is common among midlevel managers or others across nonprofits, reflecting a broader trend in the field or industry. If so, it may be important to the study, even if the study had not originally been about CSR. A good interviewer would pursue the issue with other participants, and the resulting analysis would more accurately reflect the reality of those interviewed.

NEW TYPE OF DATA. A fourth approach is following up with a new type of data. Interview researchers often combine interviews with other types of data, including large-scale surveys and ethnographic observations.[5] In our hypothetical study, the interviewer may decide to follow up by running a representative survey with questions about respondents' attitudes about CSR (or incorporating into a previously planned survey new questions on the topic).[6] They may also, instead, conduct participant observation, for example, joining in management training sessions where the company discusses corporate responsibility.[7] A less common but equally plausible alternative is to follow up by running a focus group with midlevel managers inquiring about their thoughts on CSR.

All three strategies would provide valuable new kinds of data. This kind of approach to following up is what methodologists have called "complementary mixed methods studies."[8] In such studies, one type of data is used to address the limitations of another given the particular question at hand. The most effective of such studies discuss the precise limits that one type of data will address in another. The resulting works are often quite comprehensive about the matter at hand and appropriately convincing.

NEW RESEARCH QUESTION. A fifth approach is following up with a new research question. The interview with Keith and others may have led to a deeper realization. Though the original question was how such managers conceive of their work, the interviews may have made clear that being forced to rely on for-profit corporations for nonprofit funding had created rifts between midlevel managers and their bosses. The researcher may have realized that the intriguing issue for the project to examine is not the original question—how midlevel managers conceive of their work—but the extent to which corporate trends, such as communicating to investors and the public a commitment to CSR, may produce conflicts between midlevel managers and their superiors. Attentive researchers note when interviews are telling them that their original plans are missing the more interesting, more fundamental, or otherwise more important problem.

Following up on a discovery by changing the research question takes different forms in studies with different designs. In more deductive studies, where the base questions asked of each participant are more firmly set, the researcher may simply add questions to address the new discovery. More commonly, experienced researchers in the deductive traditions know to design exploratory or preliminary interviews with a small number of respondents, who are interviewed based on a preliminary research question. Based on whatever those exploratory interviews uncover, the researcher then changes the research question. In more inductive studies, changing research questions happens several times, from the start, as each new interview follows on deeper insights gained from the previous ones until the researcher attains saturation.[9] In either case, the result is data that are far more likely to capture the important issues at play with respect to a given topic. The finished product is thus more likely to ring true to those involved and to capture more fundamental social facts.

While the five approaches are distinct, in practice, interviewers who work inductively tend to adopt several of them. One of the most common ways of doing so is when the study is aiming to attain "saturation" on a topic.[10] An interviewer attains saturation when no new interview (with the same participant or with new ones) on the topic at hand is providing information the researcher had not heard before.[11] Saturation has been especially valuable under at least two circumstances. One is when the subsequent participants were increasingly different from the ones prompting the new inquiry. If managers who are very different from Keith—with greater or lesser propensity for conflict, or of different gender or ethnic background, or in different industries, and so forth—all express some level of reservation about CSR, then it is a much safer bet that the researcher is capturing a widespread phenomenon. The other circumstance is when the interviewer has refined the research topic and therefore formulated new questions, over the course of subsequent interviews, asking about increasingly precise aspects of the topic. Over multiple interviews, the researcher would have covered exactly what aspect of CSR grates on people, whether it is more troublesome for those with lesser or with greater concern for corporate responsibility, and so forth. The resulting discussion of thoughts on CSR among managers would be far more sophisticated.

An Example

An example of the importance of following up effectively is a recent study of elite college students by Christopher Takacs.[12] Takacs's initial research question asked what value students extracted from their leadership experiences. His study ultimately exemplified several of the five approaches to following up that we have discussed. Consider his discussion of his approach: "I began my data collection with an interview study consisting of interviews with 70 students, with each student interviewed once. The interviews ranged in length from 60 to 120 minutes, were tape recorded, and later transcribed. At the start of the interview study I used an open-ended interview guide with approximately 30 questions."[13] It was a standard interview study. However, the earlier interviews yielded new issues, which he followed up on with subsequent participants (*second approach*): "As my study progressed and some of my findings began to take shape, I altered my interview guide to gather more information about new topics of particular interest."[14] His approach was highly inductive: "I followed a 'saturation' sampling method, in which I did not have a distinct number of interviews I wished to conduct at the start of the study (I anticipated anywhere from 50 to 100). As time progressed, and I found I was not gaining any new information from subsequent interviews, I altered my interview guide to focus on other topics I still wanted to explore."[15]

But Takacs found that the data he could gather from interviews alone were insufficient to address what he was discovering. So he followed up with a new type of data (*fourth approach*): "While conducting the interview study, I came to realize the limitations I faced in using only interviews to answer my research questions. Students were providing me with interesting and useful data about some areas of my project, and nearly nothing about others. I decided I needed more data, and so I added an ethnographic study to my project." He conducted participant observation of students during the extracurricular activities he had been asking about.

Over the course of interviews and ethnographic observation, Takacs uncovered that, in this elite context, students' ability to tell an interesting story about themselves was important to how they were evaluated by others, including by prospective employers. This ability, in turn, depended on access to extracurricular activities that were not equally accessible to all students. That finding was the result of shifting to a new research question (*fifth approach*): "I did not begin this study with any idea whatsoever that I would end up writing about narrative—I had initially wanted to learn about the value of student leadership experiences. The significance of narrative emerged entirely from the data as I collected [them]."[16] In the end, the author's inclination to follow the evidence wherever it led helped uncover a potential source of social inequality.

Follow-Up in Participant Observation

Because the events at a field site are unpredictable, ethnographers must continuously react to what they observe, making repeated judgments about what to pursue and what not to. Thus, they are repeatedly following up. And because ethnographers, as we have discussed, can observe any aspect of a site, its context, its people, or their interactions, the number of ways ethnographers can follow up on what they observe is probably infinite. Because ethnographers often interview people, they can adopt all of the approaches to following up we have discussed: asking new questions, conducting a new interview, turning to new participants, collecting new types of data, or changing the research question. Any of these they can do at the level of the individual or of the group. They can follow up on people or events. They can follow up on things seen, heard, felt, smelled, or touched.

Covering how all of these can be detected in the finished text is neither practical nor necessary, as the general importance of following up should, by this point, be clear: following up produces more data, strengthening the study's conclusions. However, there are two general contexts in which observers can follow up on new discoveries. Where they choose to do so, in turn, affects the finished product in somewhat different ways. A brief discussion is thus appropriate.

Two Contexts

IN THE FIELD. One context is the field site itself. Following up on what the observer uncovered in the field is, essentially, the foundation of participant observation. An observer who did not follow any lead of any kind—who never asked a question about something said, never intervened in an existing interaction, never turned a corner to see what lay beyond, or never opened a door to see where it led—would not be doing participant observation.[17] They would be doing the field equivalent of sitting behind a window in a lab, passively observing without engaging—classic nonparticipant observation. To participate in a context is to do the barest minimum of follow-up. But researchers will differ in the extent to which they have followed up, and how they do so affects which empirical claims they can make convincingly.

We have seen throughout the book that ethnographers can observe individuals, groups, interactions or other events, and physical locations, and that they can do so by focusing on any of the five senses. Any such observations, regardless of character, can be followed up on, and the result is a report of the observation that gets closer to the phenomenon at hand. Consider, as an illustration, an imagined brief excerpt from a field note written during a study of a nonprofit organization:

> While we were talking in his office, Keith's phone rang. He picked it up.
> "Hi, yes—I'm here with the researcher. [*Pause*] More CSR work? Really. [*Rolls his eyes.*] OK, you're the boss!"
> Keith hung up.

While in the field, the ethnographer could have followed up in different ways. Whether they did so effectively would depend on the empirical claim the eventual study made. For example, suppose the claim was about Keith's opinion of CSR. Following is one way the researcher could have reported it:

Keith and his boss disagreed on the value of pursuing funding from for-profit organizations looking to engage in corporate social responsibility initiatives. For example, once, while we were talking in his office, Keith's phone rang. He picked it up.

"Hi, yes—I'm here with the researcher. [*Pause*] More CSR work? Really. [*Rolls his eyes.*] OK, you're the boss!"

Keith hung up. He shook his head and continued our conversation.

The text does several of the things we have discussed as effective in ethnography, including limiting the claim to an issue for which there is evidence and reporting not a generality but a specific event (for palpability). But the lack of follow-up leaves the claim only moderately supported.

One obvious alternative is to follow up by asking, as an interviewer would. Consider how the researcher might have reported the end of that passage: "Keith hung up. When I asked why, he explained that he was not opposed to the idea of CSR; he just thought that his boss's approach just helped companies do window dressing. They weren't serious about the nonprofit's mission." But there are others.

One is to observe other events relevant to the claim. For example:

Keith hung up. Later that day, I sat in the back at a brief meeting with Keith, his boss Kamilah, and seven other workers. The third item on the agenda was CSR. When Kamilah brought it up, Keith visibly reached for his phone and started tapping on it, ignoring her. All the other workers still trained their attention quietly on the boss. When she asked if there were questions, he piped up:

"Should CSR really be our focus? We must have other options funding-wise." Sarah shook her head; Paul rolled his eyes; Kimberly took out *her* phone. Most others just slumped back into their chairs. There was an audible sigh. Kamilah explained that the issue had been settled several times before, and others nodded in agreement. The group quickly changed topics.

Following up by observing another event allowed additional evidence to enter, including the fact that Keith did not seem to have the support of others and that this issue had come up before. The ethnographer's claim that "Keith and his boss disagreed" found much stronger support. And we now understand, too, that his boss is not the only person with whom Keith disagrees.

Another way to follow up in the field is to turn to the other party in a given social interaction.

Keith hung up. The following morning, I saw his boss, Kamilah, and reminded her of where I was during the call. She immediately explained that Keith had found a way to disagree with every new initiative she introduced. Now it was CSR, but before that it was about streamlining work group assignments, and before that it was on shifting from paper to digital on routine transactions. She had learned that before she had been hired from another firm earlier in the year, he had been a favored candidate for her job. She thought the obstreperousness stemmed from resentment.

There is, again, much more evidence here in support of the empirical claim. Furthermore, we understand the reasons they disagree to greater degree and take them to mean much more. Finally, the evidence that the ethnographer followed up on increases our confidence that they did not leave stones unturned about issues relevant to the empirical claims. The work is far more convincing.

As we have said, the number of ways the ethnographer can follow up in the field is essentially infinite. And following up in the field in at least a minimal way is inevitable. The key here is that ethnographers who are alert to potentially important observations in the field are quick to find a way to follow up on them, and to do so until they have convinced themselves that the observations were either important or meaningless. This tendency is then reflected in a text where any empirical claim has multiple pieces of evidence.

OUTSIDE THE FIELD. While following up, at least minimally, is an inevitable part of participant observations, following up outside the field is not. At the end of every day in the field, the effective ethnographer writes field notes—usually many pages—that record and reflect on what was observed. Sooner or later, the researcher begins to notice patterns and must decide whether they amount to a generalization. One way of doing so is returning to the field to seek more data on those patterns. In our previous illustration, after the first call and the brief meeting, the researcher would have noticed a pattern of disagreement between Keith and his boss Kamilah. Returning to the field the next day, conversations with Kamilah confirmed and deepened the understanding of the pattern.

Another, nonexclusive way of doing follow-up involves seeking more data outside the field site. One possibility is to identify a different field site for comparison. The comparative leverage from a second site can be powerful and is the foundation of some analytical perspectives.[18] To be clear, what we are discussing is specifically turning to a second site based on what was discovered in the field during observations conducted at a first field site. As we noted earlier, an ethnographer could also have decided ahead of time to conduct fieldwork at two field sites, a perfectly appropriate strategy that would not be an example of following up. When a second field site emerges as a follow-up strategy, the most appropriate, and convincing, location would depend on the empirical claim. For example, the researcher could suspect that partnering with for-profit corporations looking to engage in CSR initiatives has become a politically charged way for nonprofit organizations to secure funding for their work. If so, then observing a second (or more) nonprofit would increase the amount of data available to evaluate the possibility. Alternatively, the researcher could suspect that male midlevel managers have seen the increase in female bosses as a threat to their upward mobility. If so, then observing other firms with increases in the proportion of women managers would bring the appropriate data to bear.

A different set of possibilities for seeking data outside the field site is to collect entirely different kinds of data. Many ethnographies are essentially mixed methods studies.[19] Among the most common practices are digging through records for archival or administrative data, to produce a historically grounded or otherwise contextualized ethnography, and conducting systematic interviews for transcript data, to produce an interview-ethnographic study.[20] Other options are conducting known-probability surveys for statistical representativeness and even running an experiment or turning to online interactions.[21] For example, the researcher might wonder whether Keith's resentment about CSR is due to its emergence and popularity. If so, they might study the history of CSR to see whether it reveals something deeper about how nonprofits have been forced to relate to their clients. Or the researcher might wonder whether Keith's attitude toward Kamilah had more to do with gender than with losing out on a promotion. If so, they might run experiments on midlevel managers in the industry to see how they assess male versus female bosses in randomly assigned scenarios.

As these examples show, following up often leads to an entirely new research question. This tendency—to follow up effectively, whether within or outside the field—is a reason that many effective ethnographies report that the question the book answered is not the one with which it began. This change is not a flaw; it is one sign of an effective researcher.

An Example

An example is Japonica Brown-Saracino's *How Places Make Us*, a study of urban life among lesbian, bisexual, and queer (LBQ) women in four US cities.[22] Brown-Saracino, a neighborhood ethnographer, was originally interested in studying how LBQ women affected gentrification. She imagined they would do so differently in different cities, so she began with a well-thought-out deductive design: "I sought to study four cities . . . that varied in terms of their place in the country, cost of living, proximity to a major city, . . . [and other variables]. I suspected that attributes, such as a city's cost of living and region, would influence gentrification dynamics and outcomes. . . . Thus, I sought two cities with long-standing LBQ populations and two with recently emerging concentrations."[23] It was a highly ambitious project for a single ethnographer, especially as the cities were spread across the country: Greenfield, MA, San Luis Obispo, CA, Portland, ME, and Ithaca, NY.

Nonetheless, she began her work alone. She explained why: "Conducting research alone in four cities prevented me from misattributing variation in findings across cities to subtle differences in method, or personality, or demographic traits, among the different ethnographers involved. By working independently, I could be certain that" the cities, not different ethnographers, were the source of any observed differences.[24] This commitment turned out to be important to the issues she followed up on.

When traveling from city to city, Brown-Saracino began to notice that she behaved differently in each place: "I slowly recognized that I was, quite literally, pulling different clothes from my suitcase in each city. In Ithaca and San Luis Obispo, I rarely considered wearing anything other than jeans. Once I got to Portland, those jeans that served me so well simply did not feel right; I found myself in skirts and dresses more than in any of the other cities."[25] Interestingly, it was not exactly on purpose. "This was not a conscious effort to blend; rather—perhaps like the people I was studying—without knowing it I was taking subtle clues from those around me about who and how to be myself in the local context."[26] Moreover, others noticed: "Indeed, I only became aware of this subtle self-adjustment when a Portland informant drew attention to my clothes. Sitting in a downtown coffee shop she asked, point blank, 'How do you identify?'"[27] The woman continued: "We've noticed that you wear a lot of skirts and dresses and that your hair is chin length, but we're not sure how you identify."[28]

It began to dawn on Brown-Saracino that, taking subtle cues from others' behavior, she had begun to act differently in each city. Moreover, others were reacting to her decisions and making inferences about her identity in the process. What she wore in each place would, whether she wanted it to or not, inevitably be a signal of her identity.

She realized that following up on this dynamic was important to understanding the experiences of LBQ women in each of the cities. Thus, her research question changed: "Recognizing, two-thirds of the way through fieldwork, the existence of place-specific identity cultures, my core research questions, pertaining to the role of LBQ migrants in gentrification, shifted substantially, calling to shift focus . . . to attend more closely to questions of identity and network."[29] She followed up by conducting extensive additional fieldwork and multiple interviews at each site. In the end, her scientific discovery was unrelated to gentrification; it was that how people express themselves is shaped subtly but unmistakably by the cities in which they live, because of how they respond to those around them.

Conclusion

Because interview and ethnographic data are co-created by the field-worker and the participants, the field-worker cannot know in advance what they will find. Following up on what is uncovered is essential to good fieldwork. Follow-up produces more data, and its significance lies in bringing more data to bear on claims that had not been anticipated. Stated differently, in qualitative research, following up is the foundation of true scientific discovery.

5 Self-Awareness

As we have argued, field-workers do not merely collect but in fact produce the data they later analyze; they co-create, in an important sense, the transcripts and field notes. We have shown throughout this book that field-workers' decisions affect many aspects of the quality of the data collected. But field-workers matter to the data collected in an even more fundamental sense: who they are—their gender, race, height and weight, level of extraversion, grace or awkwardness, hairstyle, clothing, vocabulary and intonation, class background, religion, fundamental beliefs, sympathy or disdain for others, and ignorance, and every other aspect of their identity—affects how easily they reach others, what others do and say in front of them, and how they interpret what they have heard or observed.

All of these factors shape the data themselves, and researchers differ in how cognizant they are of the consequences of this fact. That understanding, in turn, affects the quality of the final manuscript. We define self-awareness, narrowly, as the extent to which the researcher understands the impact of who they are on those interviewed and observed—and thus on the collected data. As we will see, high self-awareness is one signal of strong empirical fieldwork.

Background

Most of what we discuss under the rubric of self-awareness refers to two major ideas, one from science and another from both social and cultural studies. The first is the "observer effect," the notion that it may be impossible to observe a phenomenon without altering it. One version is the "Heisenberg effect," which, in reference to the Heisenberg uncertainty principle in physics, posits that the more precisely one determines the position of a particle, such as an electron, the less accurately one can determine the particle's speed, and vice versa.[1] Another version is the "Hawthorne effect," which refers to the tendency of people to respond to changes in their environment produced by the presence of observers.[2] The general point is that the presence of the observer inevitably affects the phenomenon observed.[3] People behave differently when they are being watched than when they are not, which affects everything from in-person surveys to laboratory experiments to both interviews and participant observation.

A more specific version of this idea is that the characteristics of the scientist collecting the data affect people's behavior. These effects have been found in a wide range of studies.[4] For example, a survey taker wearing a white laboratory coat may get a higher response rate on in-person surveys than one without the coat.[5] A woman conducting an in-person or telephone survey may hear more reports of depression, more openness to egalitarian gender roles, and more criticism of gender inequality than a male researcher.[6] An African American researcher may elicit responses from whites on opinion polls that differ from those of a white investigator, and vice versa.[7] A veiled Muslim woman surveying other Muslim women may elicit higher reports of religiosity and adherence to Islamic cultural norms than one doing so unveiled.[8] And a civilian researcher doing a ride-along to observe police officers will elicit police behavior different from that by a researcher who went through the police academy.[9] These effects derive not merely from the general state of being observed but also from the specific characteristics of those doing the observation, because existing expectations about and relations to people of different backgrounds inevitably shape how individuals act.

In an important sense, it is thus impossible for the interviewer or participant observer to capture thoughts or behavior unobtrusively. Yet the point is not that measuring behavior is doomed to failure. It is that the researcher aware of this fact reflects it in how they collect and interpret data.

A second major idea is also relevant to our concept of self-awareness. It is the notion that cultural and social analysis is less likely to fall victim to ill-conceived conclusions to the extent it is self-reflexive. A self-reflexive researcher is one who considers who they are, and their relation to those studied, as part of the research process.[10] There are many versions of this idea, with the versions differing in what they suggest is important for researchers to be aware of: their power, their position in relation to others, the standpoint informing their epistemological assumptions, the extent to which their research inadvertently contributes to inequities in the social world, and more.[11] In recent decades, some thinkers have pushed the idea further, suggesting that since all field knowledge results from the relation between the investigator and those studied, in a truly self-reflexive ethnography the researcher is ultimately the subject of investigation.[12] We do not believe that the researcher must be the object of scientific inquiry. But we will show that self-awareness about one's identity, one's relation to others, and how both affect the actions of those interviewed and observed can lead to dramatically better data and more accurate conclusions about the social world.

The scope of issues about which the author could be self-aware and the consequences of that potential awareness are both immense. We propose that the consequences are particularly important in three contexts: access, disclosure, and interpretation.

ACCESS. Some communities, groups, organizations, and individuals are more closed to outsiders than others. Elites, for example, are studied far less often than the working class and poor, because the former and their institutions are often closed to outsiders.[13] A field-worker can only study those who agree to be studied, and what we have described as the discernible elements of the researcher's identity affect how much access they will have.[14] The first element of access is the ability to enter a field site or to enter a closed group, and identity plays a role. All else being equal, it will be harder for a man than a woman to observe a sorority, for a black researcher than a white one to observe the Ku Klux Klan. But who the researcher is plays a role beyond entry. Among any set of potential participants, some field-workers—because of who they are, what they look like, what they say, or how they act—will be seen as more trustworthy than others.[15] Those who are trusted more will find that gatekeepers provide more access and that interviewees recommend others more readily.[16] Researchers aware of this fact will take it into account when seeking access.

DISCLOSURE. Related to access is disclosure. Access to a field site—getting people to talk to the researcher or to allow the observer into their spaces—is only a start. People will only express what they feel comfortable expressing, through their words or actions. They either will or will not reveal embarrassing or secret or otherwise sensitive aspects of themselves; they either will or will not allow the researcher to see them curse, make racist or sexist jokes, drink, do drugs, gamble, steal, cheat, lie to others, or do anything that might be perceived as representing them poorly.[17] And they may or may not disclose aspects of themselves in any of these ways either deliberately or unwittingly. Who the researcher is will naturally play a role, and a self-aware researcher will structure their interviews or observations, either in advance or in the interactions themselves, to maximize disclosure about the topic at hand.

INTERPRETATION. We have said that this book is focused on data collection, not on the analysis or interpretation of the data collected. But we shall see that a brief discussion of interpretation is warranted. Different researchers will interpret statements, events, and other observations differently, and all elements of their identity will naturally play a role. An observer witnessing a Catholic woman cursing at her son while in church will interpret the act as either meaningless or near blasphemous depending on their own background. A self-aware researcher will note that their first impression depends on who they are and moderate their interpretation of the event accordingly. Some qualitative scholars recommend entering the field with as little knowledge as possible of the people, places, and topics to be studied.[18] But that solution does not address that the researcher's identity, an inescapable aspect of their lives, can shape how they interpret what they uncover. As Burawoy proposes: "Remaining on the sidelines as a marginal person or positioning oneself above the 'native' not only leaves the ethnographer's own biases unrevealed and untouched but easily leads to false attributions, missing what remains implicit, what those we study take for granted."[19] Self-awareness produces manuscripts in which the researcher's potential for misreading and misinterpretation is given the attention needed for the particular matters at hand.

Self-Awareness in In-Depth Interviewing

A good interviewer can talk to anyone about any topic and elicit empirically rich and accurate information, even about difficult or sensitive parts of participants' lives. So, yes, an African American researcher can successfully interview members of a white supremacist group.[20] But that fact does not undermine the point that how much access the researcher has (before the interview), what participants disclose (during the interview), and how the researcher interprets (after the interview) what is uncovered will all be affected by who the researcher is. For any set of participants, doing any of the three successfully will be easier for some than others by virtue of their identity. We show that researchers who are self-aware in all three forms produce more empirically effective work.

Three Domains

ACCESS. To ground our discussion, consider a study of what young adults who are both LBGTQ and Catholic believe about their church's teachings on sexuality. The researcher reports the following about their methods:

Participants were recruited using a network-based sampling strategy. At the end of each interview, participants were asked to provide contact information for other potential respondents. Those potential respondents were then contacted and (if they agreed), interviewed, until the full set of participants was interviewed. This approach led to thirty-six interviews with LGBTQ young adults, of whom thirteen identified as Latino or Latina and twenty-three as white.

The passage is perfectly reasonable. But consider that access to the population of interest is not straightforward. Many LGBTQ young adults are not out to their families or other members of their community. At a minimum, a more thoughtful researcher would have acknowledged this point. For example, they could have added the following: "All of my respondents were publicly out before the interview. For this reason, my study does not discuss the experiences of an important part of the population, those uncomfortable or unwilling to be public about their sexuality." Or alternatively, "While most of my respondents were out to close friends, not all of them were out publicly. The study likely underreports the experiences of those least public about their sexuality." There are many other alternatives. The point is that the original passage, as stated, ignored a glaringly important constraint to access that affects the scientific conclusions.

But access is not just affected by the respondents' sexuality. The topic and specific subpopulation of LGBTQ adults play a role as well because of their church's formal position on homosexuality. Consider the official catechism of the Catholic Church: "Basing itself on Sacred Scripture, which presents homosexual acts as acts of grave depravity, tradition has always declared that 'homosexual acts are intrinsically disordered'. They are contrary to the natural law. . . . Under no circumstances can they be approved."[21] Local communities will differ in their interpretation of the totality of the Catholic Church's teachings on sexuality, but a thoughtful researcher would consider them when seeking access, and reflect that consideration in their report. For example, the following could be added: "Most participants were from a large California community in which Catholic church leaders have openly espoused progressive values and criticized some of the positions of the Church. Most participants were open about their sexuality and regularly attended mass. Findings would likely differ in more conservative social contexts." Again, there are many alternatives. Acknowledgment by the researcher that the topic itself would affect access, and thus the likely conclusions, would signal a stronger study.

Nevertheless, none of these improved reports would reflect "self-awareness" as we use the term. The issue is that who the researcher is plays a role as well. For this particular topic, whether the researcher is LGBTQ or not, or Catholic or not, would likely matter. Respondents might (or might not) be more reluctant to talk to non-LGBTQ or non-Catholic interviewers; they might (or might not) fear that Catholic non-LGBTQ researchers might be uncomfortable with their sexuality; they might (or might not) fear that a non-Catholic LGBTQ respondent might be judgmental about their faith. These issues would affect who is willing to talk. They might also affect who participants are willing to recommend, which would alter the results of the snowballing strategy.

However, the point is not that the researcher would need to be an LGBTQ Catholic; as we discuss later, that background might produce its own issues. The point is that being unaware about these issues means that the researcher did nothing to address them when seeking access. Consider what a more self-aware researcher might have done.

When recruiting participants for this study, I used a snowball approach, beginning with my personal networks. As a child, I went to mass every Sunday with my family, played basketball on Catholic youth league teams, and joined the church youth group. Almost everyone in my community was Chicano, as I am. My first interviewees were two friends from my high school years, a gay Guatemalan and a white lesbian now in their early thirties. I was one of the first heterosexual persons either of them had come out to. When we reconnected, I explained that I attended mass less often, and that I am more critical of the church than I was as a boy. After the interview, I asked them to recommend other LGBTQ Catholics. They each named two people, and I asked each to let me know how public the referred people were about their sexuality before contacting them. After each interview, I repeated this process. This approach led to thirty-six interviews with LGBTQ young adults, of whom thirteen identified as Latino or Latina and twenty-three as white. Most were out to close friends; about half were not public about their sexuality beyond close friends.

The researcher is clearly far more self-aware, recognizing that his background and connection to the initial participants (the "seeds") in the network will matter for his access to others. He is also aware that his own sexuality may affect access. And he is aware that, since people differ in how open they are about their sexuality, approaching people with the presumption that they are out might induce anxiety in his participants or expose them to community reprobation. Self-awareness includes recognition of the potential of causing harm.

A non-Catholic might have adopted a different strategy and still reflected self-awareness.

When recruiting participants for this study, I used a snowball approach. Because I knew little about Catholicism, I first studied the church's positions on sexuality and other issues, attended mass several times (without taking communion), and spoke to priests in three parishes. One priest recommended two parishioners who often talked about social issues; I interviewed both of them about a broad range of topics, explaining the focus of my study. Each of them explained that they did not know the sexuality of people in their parish but could recommend others to talk to about social issues broadly. The sixth person I interviewed eventually confided that he was gay and then asked me if I had ever been with a man. I said I had not. "Then why are you writing this book?" he asked. I explained my interest in people facing morally complicated situations. He—technically the first participant in the study—referred me to other gay Catholics in his network, explaining that because most of them were closeted, he would have them call me if they were interested. From there, I snowballed, asking each respondent to recommend two people. This approach led to thirty-six interviews with LGBTQ young adults, of whom thirteen identified as Latino or Latina and twenty-three as white. Most were out to close friends; about half were not public about their sexuality beyond close friends.

The reader, again, has far more information about access. The researcher reflected awareness, and self-awareness, about several of the same important issues. He also made clear how his outsider status, a potential obstacle to access, was overcome.

DISCLOSURE. Most of the aspects of who the researcher is that affect access also shape what people are willing to disclose. And researchers who are self-aware about access (before the interview) are usually self-aware about disclosure (during the interview). But successful access does not guarantee self-awareness during the interview itself. Many researchers get lucky. For example, a former Catholic entirely lacking in self-awareness might recall that among his high school friends were a Latino who was gay and a white lesbian, who themselves may open doors out of camaraderie or nostalgia. Or the particular community of interest may not be difficult to access. Or the researcher may have access to funds that pay participants sufficiently strong compensation to ensure a large pool of interviews. In any of these contexts, a researcher lacking self-awareness would experience the consequences during the interview itself.

Psychologists and interviewers have written at length about the factors that shape disclosure during the interview.[22] We refer readers to those works for an extended discussion. Here we limit ourselves to two points specific to disclosure and self-awareness.

First, one cannot successfully replace self-awareness with demographic matching.[23] Some researchers believe people should interview only those of the same race, class, or other demographic background. Analogously, but less radically, some large-scale research projects enlist interviewers who match the demographic characteristics of respondents for studies about issues involving those characteristics. For example, for a large study of married couples, they might hire women to interview women and men to interview men; for a study of race discrimination, they might hire same-race interviewers for each of the given racial groups; or for a study of LGBTQ Catholics, they might hire only LGBTQ Catholic interviewers. Such decisions might or might not be a good idea for a given topic. But doing so does not reduce the significance of self-awareness. For example, a gay Catholic who has lived his whole life in a large progressive parish in California may mistakenly expect similar openness in Boston, turning off respondents interpersonally, resulting in reticence and discretion on their part. Only self-awareness provides the benefits of self-awareness. Identity, to the extent it is important to the interview, is not just a summation of a person's race, class, gender, sexuality, and religion; it is a multifaceted component of the self, including background, personal history, demeanor, modes of self-expression, and more.

Second, from the perspective of disclosure, demographic matching can bring advantages and disadvantages. Consider a case in which demographic matching might be justified. A researcher is interested in studying how people approach family planning and is specifically targeting those lesbian and gay Catholic young adults who are not out to their parents and other relatives. The researcher is Catholic, lesbian, and in her early thirties; she hires a gay Catholic in his early twenties, and they each interview only participants of the same gender. The advantages are clear. Researchers have shown that people are willing to confide personal matters to those who can empathize with their situation.[24] Given the explicit position that the Catholic Church has taken on marriage among same-sex partners, it is reasonable to expect that participants will believe a Catholic of the same gender and sexual orientation who is of family planning age is more likely to understand these particular issues. That set of conditions would suggest they might disclose more. But similarity is a double-edged sword. Researchers have also shown that people do not express things they believe should be obvious to an interlocutor, because it does not occur to them, or they believe it might come across as patronizing, or they presume both parties understand that it does not need to be said.[25] If so, they might disclose less.

For any given study, whether people will disclose less or more can only be known in the field. But in the absence of self-awareness, a researcher will have a difficult time addressing the potential problems with either matching demographically or not doing so. Further, the researcher may not notice that the participant has not disclosed something important. A female interviewer may be unaware that her gay Catholic respondents are uncomfortable discussing sexual issues openly with someone of the opposite sex. Conversely, a gay Catholic interviewer who has not yet been intimate with other men may be unaware that his gay Catholic respondents do not bother discussing several sexual issues they wrongly assume he has already experienced. Indeed, studies that do not report any issues with potential disclosure are likely to have faced disclosure problems. Not addressing the issue is a common sign that lack of self-awareness has affected the quality of the data.

INTERPRETATION. Self-awareness matters not only before or during the interview but also after. The key point is simple: researchers lacking self-awareness will misinterpret the data. It is certainly the case that general awareness is important to interpretation. The interviewer must have a sense of what local terms, slang, symbolic references, and other culturally specific elements may be playing a role in what the interviewer says. The non-Catholic would want to have studied Catholicism before interpreting data, lest they arrive at the wrong conclusions. But self-awareness is distinctly important to the interpretation process, and lacking it can play a role even if it did not during recruitment or in the interview itself.

Consider an example. The interviewer identifies as lesbian and grew up Catholic but has not attended mass in a few decades. She approaches LBQ Catholic young women in Boston who are publicly out; she has no problems with access, and interviewees open up to her. She interviews Emma, who eschews labels and is in a serious relationship with a woman, one Monday in late August.

INTERVIEWER: Have you talked to your parents about getting serious with Ava?

EMMA: You know how it is with Catholics. I try to avoid it. I have a problem with the Church, my dad, with all of them. I don't want to be subordinate to anyone. My dad is the worst—he liked Robert but hates Ava. I'll always be Catholic, I'll always go to mass, but I'll do things my own way. Robert was wicked controlling, anyway, especially during COVID. With Ava there is none of that stuff. We're happy.

The researcher reports the following: "Emma tended to avoid discussing her same-sex relationships with her parents. She particularly did not like being 'subordinate' to her father, who was domineering." The researcher's interpretation would seem perfectly plausible. But Emma, like many respondents, said many things at once, and an entirely different alternative is reasonable.

Knowing the researcher was Catholic, Emma may have assumed that, like every Catholic in her circle, the interviewer was at mass the previous Sunday, the fourth Sunday in August of that year. On any given day, all Catholic churches follow the same script during liturgy. Assuming the interviewer had been to mass, Emma would have made reference to the following: "Brothers and sisters: / Be subordinate to one another out of reverence for Christ. / Wives should be subordinate to their husbands as to the Lord.... / As the church is subordinate to Christ, / so wives should be subordinate to their husbands in everything."[26] The researcher, unaware that Emma believed her to be more devout than she was, misinterpreted Emma's reference.

Interpretation is generally a feature of the analysis, not data collection, phase of the research process, and thus is largely outside of the scope of this book. However, it is worth discussing here, because flaws in interpretation can sometimes point to mishaps in data collection. Note that, in the preceding illustration, the misinterpretation could have been addressed with greater self-awareness when the data were being collected, at the point of the interview, wherein the participant might have disclosed more. For example, an effective interviewer would have made Emma aware of her own, less committed approach to Catholicism, which likely would have led to a different interview.

INTERVIEWER: Have you talked to your parents about getting serious with Ava?

EMMA: You know how it is with Catholics. I try to avoid it. I have a problem with the Church, my dad, with all of them. I don't want to be subordinate to anyone. I know you said you don't go to mass anymore, but last Sunday the priest talked about Ephesians, the stuff about subordinating yourself to your husband like the church does to Christ. Anyway, I don't agree with that at all, and my dad doesn't either, but he still doesn't think it's a big deal. I'll always be Catholic, I'll always go to mass, but I'll do things my own way. Robert was wicked controlling, anyway, especially during COVID. I don't know why my dad liked Robert but hates Ava. With Ava there is none of that stuff. We're happy.

Thoughtfulness about the self inevitably improves the quality of interview data. And self-awareness at the disclosure stage can help ward off interpretation issues at the interpretation stage.

An Example

For our example, we briefly show the importance of self-awareness to gaining access to a population before interviews begin. Consider Karida Brown's *Gone Home*, a study of how African Americans managed race relations and politics in Appalachia.[27] The author interviewed members of many families across generations to understand how the people of this coal-mining region had changed after deindustrialization.

Brown was aware that her own background played a role in her ability to access others in an area known for distrust of outsiders. "I am a third-generation descendent of this population," she explained.[28] "My mother and father were both born and reared in Lynch, Kentucky, and they subsequently migrated to Long Island, New York, where they raised my brother and me. My earliest childhood memories include pilgrimages 'back home' to the mountains during Memorial Day weekend as well as what seemed at the time to be exotic voyages to the Eastern Kentucky Social Club (EKSC) Reunions."[29]

But her access was not a mere function of demographic background or family history. It was, in fact, the opening of doors: "The visit [returning to Kentucky for a family reunion after twelve years away] was so familiar. It was as though no time had passed. Every person that I greeted while walking the streets knew exactly who I belonged to: 'There goes a Brown!' or 'You must be a Davis; Nita's girl, right?' That's just how intimate and close-knit the community is there, even in the forty-year aftermath of mass out-migration."[30]

Nevertheless, she is aware, too, of the fact that she is by no means a full insider, not merely because many years have passed since her visit but also because the place has changed:

> [The visit] brought back so many happy memories from my childhood visits when my grandparents were still living. However, the state of the place itself was jarring. The built environment of the towns looked half the size of what I remembered from a little over a decade ago. So many homes were torn down or rotting in ruins. And although there were plenty of people there for the weekend, it was markedly fewer than how it used to be.[31]

The author was clearly self-aware about her relationship to those she was about to study and was explicit about its role in her access to participants.

Self-Awareness in Participant Observation

Self-awareness is no less important to the ethnographer. The ethnographer must establish rapport to enter a group, site, or community;

communicate the trust required for people to interact as normal; and interpret what is observed, both immediately while taking field notes and much later while analyzing the data, with awareness of the ethnographer's impact on the process. Many of the issues are directly analogous to those in the interview process, but some different dynamics are at play.

Three Domains

ACCESS. Imagine an ethnographic study of the relationship between religion and politics wherein the author conducted regular observations of religious services and activities at two Catholic churches. The author describes the process as follows:

> I selected two churches for observation, both located in greater Chicago. St. Charles served a primarily white suburban community; St. Patrick, a predominantly Latino semirural community. I attended a Sunday morning or Saturday evening mass at each site almost every week for one year. I also attended mass at all Holy Days of Obligation during the period, and other community activities. After mass, I usually hung around in the back of the church, chatting with parishioners and with the priests and deacons, resulting in more than 550 hours of exposure. I recorded my observations in field notes, which I almost always wrote within 24 hours of each visit.

The passage is perfectly reasonable. It also provides important details about the quality of the data, including the total hours of exposure. However, the only thing it says about how the author attained access is that they attended mass, leaving open the extent to which a lack of self-awareness might have affected whom or what sites the researcher had accessed and why.

A more self-aware researcher might have added the following: "In each research site, after my first time at mass, I first approached the priest, explaining that I was writing a book on how churches help their congregants understand contemporary issues. I mentioned in those conversations that I am Catholic, that I was a choir boy, and that I still attend mass regularly." The reader has a clearer sense of how the researcher's religious background affected access.

The researcher could do more. Access is not a given, even for Catholics, and some communities are skeptical of researchers. An even more self-aware researcher might have discussed the issue thus:

The priest at St. Patrick seemed skeptical of my intentions. He never responded to my initial email requesting a meeting, so I attended the Spanish mass one Sunday morning and then stuck around afterward to chat with him. I began the conversation in tentative Spanish. The priest, a Latino, followed my lead at first but then quickly switched to English, so I did the same. He explained that, while I was welcome in the church, his responsibility is "to the community." Gesturing at a few families talking and laughing at the rear of the church, he explained: "Our parishioners feel safe here. I don't want anything to jeopardize that." That same polite but wary welcome extended to other church leaders and parishioners, most of whom were Latino. After each Spanish mass at St. Patrick I attended, I tried to strike up a conversation (often in Spanish) with other attendees, and it took me almost two months of regular visits to find anyone other than the priest who would respond with more than a quick nod and hello.

The passage is very illuminating. First, we get a clear sense that the researcher is aware that he does not inherently inspire trust. Second, by being explicit that his interactions with several people revealed their mistrust, he made clear that the issue not only was limited to one priest but was a feature of either the community or his relationship to it.

But the passage also reveals one of the most common forms of lack of self-awareness, perhaps the single most predictable feature of a budding ethnographer's field notes in predominant groups. It reports everyone's ethnic background but his own. In our example, the researcher happens to be white, but his failure to be explicit about the fact reveals an understanding of whiteness as a default category—his own race is so obvious it does not need, in his mind, to be stated. A more self-aware researcher would have revealed his own ethnic background, which might have paved the way for a more thoughtful discussion of the role of the researcher's background in access.

> [I] then stuck around after to chat with him. I began the conversation in Spanish, a language I had more or less learned after six years in school and one college year spent in Mexico. The priest, a Latino, followed my lead at first but then quickly switched to English, so I did the same. He explained that, while I was welcome in the church, his responsibility is "to the community." Gesturing at a few families talking and laughing at the rear of the church, he explained: "Our parishioners feel safe here. I don't want anything to jeopardize that." I am a white, U.S.-born, Italian American, and I was not sure if his statement about "safety" was a reference to all outsiders, to white ones, or to people who might expose parishioners to the Department of Homeland Security, since the rate

of undocumented migrants was high in this outer suburb of Chicago. The priest's same polite but wary welcome extended to other church leaders and parishioners, most of whom were Latino.

We now know his native language and where he learned Spanish—we have a clearer description than the ambiguous phrase "tentative Spanish," which could have referred to either the quality of his Spanish or his demeanor. Even more importantly, we now know not only his race but also his country of birth, which together provide potential clues about what the priest, and the rest of the community, seemed apprehensive about. The researcher would need to say more, but the path is certainly the right one, and the reader has much greater confidence in the author.

DISCLOSURE. Most of what we have discussed so far applies to what people are willing to disclose. We need not belabor the point. The one issue worth adding is that disclosure involves not merely what people say but also what they do, and a self-aware researcher would take note of that fact. Consider, as an illustration, the same ethnographic study:

> By my eighth or ninth week in the field, the number of parishioners at St. Patrick had risen from about fifty to more than seventy-five. I had started counting on my second visit, and the numbers had only begun to rise at week six. I spent several weeks wondering what had made the services more popular. The priest had not changed, and neither had his approach to services. I could not identify any change in migration patterns in the community, as the harvest had long passed, and the seasonal work, if anything, was declining. By now, people were much more open with me, at times

even approaching me to say hello. It began to dawn on me that my presence might have affected attendance, so I made concerted efforts to reveal more about myself—my interests, my background, the ideas I was developing for the book. Carmen, a parishioner who had become a key informant, noticed my greater openness, and endorsed it. During my first site visit, she explained, people saw me talking with the priest and attempting to approach other parishioners, which led to speculation that I was some kind of official. According to Carmen, a number of regular attendees decided to skip mass beginning the next week or attend alternate services. It took a while for the rumors to die down—but they did. By the third month, I was invited to my first of three *quinceañeras*.

As the passage makes clear, the field-worker's presence can affect not only what people say but also what they do. In this case, it affected both access and disclosure, whom he saw and what they did. The researcher was alert enough to uncover this fact and to react accordingly. His greater openness—his understanding that how much they trust him depends on how much they know him—improved how much they disclosed about themselves over the course of their natural interactions, in family gatherings and festivities.

INTERPRETATION. Interpretation matters in all the ways expected per the analogous discussion in the context of interviews. Consider the example. For the first eight weeks of fieldwork, many parishioners in essence disappeared. All of the data he collected until then were from those selectively more trusting members of the parish, from people within the community, who were more comfortable confiding in others and disclosed more of themselves than the average person. The researcher's eventual awareness of this fact would shape how he, and in turn we, interpret the reported data.

Two more issues are worth noting. First, one particularly important question in participant observation involves harm. Many ethnographic studies occur at sites, or among populations, where safety is important. Researchers must of course be cognizant of ensuring their own safety. But they must also take care not to inadvertently harm those studied, an issue that comes into play during the interpretation, and later presentation, of the data. If St. Patrick were, in fact, a parish with a high proportion of undocumented migrants, high exposure could make the area a target of immigration raids. A full discussion of the ethics involved in writing up results lies beyond the scope of this book. However, we note that, to follow our previous example, a researcher lacking awareness may correctly note that some aspect of who he was had affected how others were relating to him, while at the same time neglecting that his reporting of that fact confirmed their suspicions, for he had carelessly exposed the parishioners to scrutiny. The importance of self-awareness does not end at the field site.

Second, an important issue involves narrative. We have seen that passages that demonstrate self-awareness in the context of access, disclosure, or interpretation tend to be longer. They are also self-reflexive in the sense that the authors, in our illustrations, have often talked about themselves. However, researchers need not talk extensively about themselves to demonstrate self-awareness, and some qualitative researchers say a lot about themselves without revealing much self-awareness about how others are reacting to their presence. The key here, as in any scientific endeavor, is the people studied, not the researcher. A critical perspective on the self need not imply that the aim is autobiography. The aspects of the researcher's background or personality that are important to what we describe as self-awareness are those that directly affect how people respond to that researcher.

An Example

An example of the value of self-awareness for effective access to a population can be found in Carol Stack's classic study of family support networks in an African American urban neighborhood she called "The Flats."[32] In the very first sentence of the book's introduction, Stack not only made clear that her own identity had affected her access but also revealed her race and age, which turned out to be important: "This introduction anticipates curiosity about how a young white woman could conduct a study of black family life, and provides a basis for evaluating the reliability and quality of the data obtained."[33] She continued, in ways that echo much of our discussion: "The questions raised relate to a broad spectrum of questions fundamental to social analysis. Is it possible for an outsider who symbolizes the dominant culture to enter a black community, win the community's participation and approval, acquire reliable data, and judge its reliability?"[34] In that passage, the author expressly pointed to the importance of self-awareness to access, disclosure, and interpretation. She was aware that her identity and how others would respond to it matter.

Stack went on to directly discuss access: "I could have gained my first contacts in The Flats by working through the established network of black men and women who had status and power in the [neighborhood and the larger community]."[35] She feared, however, that the combination of who they were and who she was would limit her access to a particular subset of the population, those deemed by a subset of leaders to be somehow acceptable to white outsiders. "I decided instead to find my own means of entrée.... Through my own efforts and good luck I came to know a young woman who had grown up on welfare in The Flats and had since come to my university. She agreed to introduce me to families she had known as she was growing up there. She would introduce me to two unrelated families and from then on I would be on my own."[36]

Stack did much more. When she first met one of the families that turned out to be a focus of observation, she sat with them in their living room and helped them fold newspapers for one of the children's evening paper route. The work took an hour or two and turned out to be an important signal to the participants of Stack's trustworthiness as a researcher. She wrote that after finishing, "I told them I would like to begin a study of family life in The Flats. [They] told me to come by again and bring my baby. Several months later [the mother] told me that she had been surprised that I sat with them that first day to fold papers, and then came back to help again. 'White folks', she told me, 'don't have time, they's always in a rush, and they don't sit on black folk's furniture, at least no whites that come into The Flats.'"[37]

Stack understood that several aspects of her identity would affect access to the community and quickly found evidence of the fact. She adopted an entry strategy that avoided some of the difficulties involved, such as being introduced only to specific subsets of the population. And she worked early to earn the trust of a population who had learned to distrust many people like her. Her work provided many reasons to believe that lack of self-awareness was unlikely to be a major problem. Stack is a masterful ethnographer, and we refer readers to her work for examples of many of the topics we have discussed in this book.

Conclusion

The identity of the field-worker—with the term "identity" broadly understood—affects who they can reach, how effectively they can do so, and how they make sense of the results. A self-aware researcher considers this fact before, during, and after the data collection process. And an astute one ensures that the reader understands the researcher's self-awareness.

Conclusion

We have proposed that the scientific merit of a study based on in-depth interviews or participant observation can be assessed by its degree of cognitive empathy, heterogeneity, palpability, follow-up, and self-awareness. These criteria are not exhaustive. Nor do they cover every aspect important to a qualitative study; they largely center on data collection, not design, analysis, or theory, all of which also matter. But these criteria are fundamental to effective data collection, which is the basis of any successful empirical study. And they are among the most distinctive elements of strong craft in qualitative research, the aspects of such work that make it indispensable to the scientific enterprise.

Qualitative research is diverse. Researchers disagree on both broad epistemological questions, such as whether fieldwork should be approached deductively or inductively (or abductively), and narrow design questions, such as how many respondents should be interviewed. They will likely disagree on these matters for many years to come. But despite their disagreements, experienced field-workers tend to agree on whether a researcher, once in the field, interviewed or observed others effectively; on whether the interviewer elicited deep and meaningful data; or on whether the ethnographer detected elements of a site, context, or set of interactions likely to matter to the topic at hand. Experienced field-workers, we insist, can detect high craftsmanship in one another's work. What they detect is the very heart of what qualitative research brings to science, those elements of the social world that cannot be captured except by asking questions effectively over a long period of trust building or by observing thoughtfully and astutely over a long period of immersion. But what they detect is rarely articulated, instead being passed down quietly in offices and hallways from advisers to their students, or else discovered anew by each successive generation of field-workers. We believe that articulating these issues and bringing them to light is essential to the scientific enterprise.

Bringing these issues to light is important for both insiders and outsiders. Much of today's qualitative research is addressing questions that, because they involve contemporary problems—such as inequality, poverty, education, discrimination, polarization, health, immigration, management, and policy—are also being examined by quantitative researchers. As a result, whereas ethnographers in the past could be content knowing that their evaluators would be other ethnographers, today's field researchers are inevitably producing work being read and evaluated by economists, demographers, psychologists, quantitative sociologists, statisticians, and others who are experts on the subject matter but not on method. Everyone must be clear, we argue, on how to evaluate the work. Such clarity is particularly important amid the current crisis of public confidence in the social sciences as a whole.

Our Perspective

Our position is that qualitative research is essential to a cumulative social science, that fulfilling its potential requires being clear on assessment standards, that one key to clarifying those standards is distinguishing approaches to data analysis from methods of data collection, and—perhaps most importantly—that whether a study's methods of data collection were effective should be evaluated based on whether it accomplishes what the methods are intended to do. In-depth interviews are intended to capture how people understand themselves and their circumstances; participant observation, to directly observe phenomena in their natural contexts. One can do either of them well or poorly. We have aimed to explain how to tell the difference.

The two methods of data collection share the fact that the researcher not only collects data per a prior expectation but in fact produces the data, in the field, as a function of decisions made in the moment about what to probe or not probe—about what to inquire about or not, observe or not pay attention to, and take or not take notes on. The researcher's in-the-field decisions shape the very nature of the data collected, and their words and actions are inextricably part of the data. Two researchers interviewing the same person, or observing the same field site, will thus inevitably produce different data, different transcripts and field notes. This difference constitutes the core predicament for qualitative projects that aim to produce cumulative science.

We have asserted that in spite of this difference, and although the resulting transcripts or field notes will differ, two hypothetical researchers can arrive at the same social facts about those interviewed or observed. In fact, if both researchers are skilled at their craft, they are likely to do so, provided they have enough exposure. Exposure is thus the precondition of strong empirical qualitative research. Without exposure—without many hours interviewing participants or observing field sites—empirically strong fieldwork is impossible.

Evaluation

For this reason, a reader evaluating a qualitive empirical project that follows the principles outlined in this book would first assess exposure. Time exposed in the field is the sine qua non. A project with little exposure is empirically dead on arrival.

Assuming sufficient exposure, the reader would look for signs of cognitive empathy, which is among the primary objects of most empirical projects in the study of social problems. The reader would assess whether, at a minimum, the narrative reported how those interviewed or observed perceive themselves and their social world. The evidence would be palpable or concrete, rather than abstract or general. The narrative in general would depict heterogeneity. If it showed little diversity across people, over time, among situations, or between contexts in any central aspect of the findings—if a single empirical pattern were reported repeatedly, with little variation—then the work would be deeply suspect. Heterogeneity would signal that the researcher had interviewed and observed with at least minimal judiciousness.

Those are bare minimums. A stronger narrative would exhibit cognitive empathy not only about how people perceive the world but also about what meaning they attach to those perceptions and, if relevant, what motives they express for their actions.

It would likely report heterogeneity in meanings and (if relevant) motivations as well, and probably explain why the meanings people gave to things differed. And because good fieldwork responds to the unexpected, the researchers would have followed up on unanticipated statements or observations. In fact, a common sign of strong ethnographies is that the author reports answering a research question different from the one with which they started. The stronger narrative, finally, would reveal an author explicitly aware of the impact of their presence on who was accessed and what they disclosed.

The indicators we have reported here are elementary, in the sense that they refer to what one can see in the finished project if the researcher, at the level of basic craft, executed the data collection competently. Beyond these indicators, perspectives will differ. For example, some scholars will argue that the number of respondents will matter, and others that it will not. Some will argue that longitudinal data collection is important, and others that it is not. Some will argue that testing hypotheses is essential, and others that generating theory from the ground up is the objective. Some will insist on the need for comparative cases, and others will point to the long history of single-case studies.

Addressing all of these issues would require an entire volume. Nonetheless, we stress the importance of two assumptions that have informed the main arguments of this book. First, except for a high level of exposure, no design feature is necessary for all interview studies or for all participant observation studies to be empirically effective. While this proposition might seem obvious, some researchers disagree. For example, some researchers insist that all interview-based studies must have some minimal number of interviewees (an idea derived from sampling methods in survey research).[1] Similarly, some researchers insist that all ethnographies must have at least two comparative cases (an idea derived from the notion of treatment and control groups in experiments).[2] We believe such perspectives ignore that different studies have different objectives, and the objectives may call for different designs. An interview study with many survey-like questions that aims to make a claim about the distribution of a given known variable in the population as a whole will need a sufficiently large sample selected from an appropriate sampling frame in which all respondents are selected with known probability. An interview study that aims to understand a hitherto unknown phenomenon—to uncover so-called unknown unknowns—in very small and difficult-to-reach but important populations (e.g., the very first Wuhan residents with COVID-19) will need a sufficiently targeted approach wherein accuracy and saturation will be essential and statistical representativeness an irrelevant criterion. Similarly, an ethnographic study that seeks to compare some existing feature in two organizations will certainly need to select both; one that seeks to uncover how an important community changed after an event (e.g., the city of New Orleans after Hurricane Katrina) will need to ensure sufficient years of fieldwork to capture the short- and long-run consequences, such that time at the site will be essential and comparison an irrelevant criterion. There are infinitely more possible kinds of questions and an equally large number of plausible alternative designs.

Second, all methods of data collection should be evaluated fundamentally on the basis of what they are designed to do. Because any given study has many components, it can be assessed in multiple ways. But no method can be reasonably critiqued on the basis of something for which it was not intended. For example, a particular survey-based study can be assessed on the basis of many criteria. But to criticize surveys as methods of data collection on the basis that they cannot, say, capture behavior unobtrusively, is to misunderstand the objectives of surveys. Similarly, to criticize in-depth interview studies or participant observation studies as methods of data collection on the bases of sample size (as opposed to exposure), controlled design, or any other core criterion that is not fundamental to their strengths is to misunderstand the objectives of each method. Our book has aimed to make clear how to assess interviewing and participant observation on the basis of what they were intended to do.

And what they are intended to do is indispensable to social science. Just as science needs some scholars to design experiments in a controlled laboratory, others to conduct randomized control trials in the field, and others to describe the characteristics of total populations with confidence, it needs some to talk to people; convincingly earn their trust; and elicit believable statements about how the people perceive themselves and the world, find meaning in it, and motivate their actions. It needs some to gain access to communities, groups, villages, neighborhoods, and organizations; become accepted as observers; and accurately, reflectively, and comprehensively report on the interactions and actions taking place. We have shown the reader, we hope, how to determine whether those interviewers and ethnographers have done their jobs well.

Acknowledgments

This book began as a lecture given by Mario in 2018 on the importance of qualitative literacy to a democratic society, part of the Coming to Terms with a Polarized Society Series of the Institute for Social and Economic Research and Policy at Columbia University. Mario again gave the address at the 2019 American Education Research Association meeting as its Spencer Foundation Lecture. We thank ISERP and the Spencer Foundation for the opportunity to introduce and discuss these ideas. For the second lecture, Mario discussed in positive terms the empirical work of Jessica, whom he had met once but not worked with previously. After the lecture, the two of us decided, after several months of discussing our common interest in field methods and exploring possible projects, to write a short book on how to evaluate qualitative research. The task was a lot harder than either of us had anticipated. After drafting the book, we shared each of the main chapters with the authors of works highlighted therein as examples, in hopes that we were not misquoting anyone too egregiously. We thank Karida Brown, Japonica Brown-Saracino, Andrew Deener, Cayce Hughes, Jennifer Lee, Danielle Raudenbush, Chris Takacs, Celeste Watkins-Hayes, and Min Zhou for indulging us and for providing helpful comments and critiques. We also thank Elizabeth Bruch, D'Lane Compton, Tara García Mathewson, Kathleen Gerson, Monika Krause, Nicholas Lemann, Dick Murnane, Steve Raudenbush, and Bel Willem for conversations or comments on everything from the book's title to the entire manuscript. Though none of these people deserve blame for anything we assert, they all deserve credit for helping us clarify our thinking.

Naomi Schneider was enthusiastic about this book from the beginning, and we are grateful. Last but certainly not least, we thank Dan and Tara for doing more than their share of childcare while we pushed to finalize the manuscript, and to Arabella, Layla, Leo, and Odin for their patience, hours of entertainment, and inspiration.

A Note on Proposals

The question animating this book was how to distinguish a sound piece of empirical qualitative research from something that was not, from a work that was, say, beautifully written but empirically unsound. Some readers will want to distinguish sound from unsound work not in a finished book or paper but in one being proposed. Evaluating qualitative proposals is increasingly common among the major foundations, both federal (such as NSF and NIH) and private (such as William T. Grant and Russell Sage), that finance social science research. Since we share those foundations' aims of supporting high-quality, empirical social science based on interviews or participant observation, it seems prudent to comment on the evaluation of proposals.

A Challenge

Using our criteria to evaluate proposals is difficult, for at least three reasons. First, our criteria distinguish empirical soundness in completed work based on the quality of the collected data. A proposal to conduct empirical research has not yet produced the data that our guidelines are meant to evaluate. Second, while proposals are often evaluated on their research design, our book has explicitly focused on execution (in the field), not conception (in the office), and design is an element of conception. As we noted in chapter 1, we did not discuss design, or conception more generally, because the range of issues to be covered and the number of disagreements to resolve are both far greater than can be addressed within a short book.

Third, our criteria acknowledge a reality that many evaluators find uncomfortable, which is that not all field-workers base their work on what quantitative scholars would consider a "research design." Field-workers vary. Some of them, before conducting a single interview or observation, study the literature, generate hypotheses, define their variables, create a sampling frame, compile extensive interview guides, and specify complete coding schemes. Others eschew strict hypotheses before entering the field; they decide only on a research question, a field site or population, and an initial plan, then finalize the details in the field, in response to emerging findings. Still others do not even formalize a research question; they begin only with a topic—such as gender relations among employees in a firm or support networks among kin in a neighborhood—and seek to uncover unknown unknowns in a chosen field site. In fact, many participant observers have no a priori design to speak of, only a commitment to follow up systematically on emerging discoveries related to the topic of interest. There are many other variations in approaches.

Unlike in other methods, there is no necessary relationship between the extensiveness of the design and the quality of the finished product. This difference from other methods is important. An experiment that has not been explicitly designed—with variables, treatments, and procedures clearly specified—cannot produce good science, because an experiment is not inductive in nature.[1] Yet many of the most scientifically important ethnographic studies were not explicitly research designed.[2] The eminent ethnographer Howard Becker made the point forcefully in his critique of two reports by the National Science Foundation on how to evaluate qualitative proposals.[3] He wrote:

> Inspection of the research classics . . . shows that [many] researchers don't fully specify methods, theory or data when they begin their research. They start out with ideas, orienting perspectives, even specific hypotheses, but once they begin they investigate new leads, apply useful theoretical ideas to the (sometimes unexpected) evidence they gather, and in other ways conduct a systematic and rigorous scientific investigation. Each interview and each day's observations produce ideas tested against relevant data. Not fully prespecifying these ideas and procedures, and being ready to change them when their findings require it, is not a flaw, but rather one of the great strengths of qualitative research.[4]

For Becker, the key is that much of qualitative research is necessarily iterative: "Successful qualitative research is an iterative process, one in which the data gathered at T1 inform data gathering operations conducted at T2. Successful researchers recognize that they begin their work knowing very little about their object of study, and that they use what they learn from day to day to guide their subsequent decisions about what to observe, who to interview, what to look for, and what to ask about."[5]

The consequence is that specifying how to evaluate a proposal is easier in other data collection methods than in in-depth interviewing or participant observation, because in the qualitative methods the specificity of the design is not necessarily related to the quality of the finished product. For those approaches to in-depth interviewing that more closely resemble surveys, the design will matter most; for those that do not—that require openness because, for example, they are studying a topic or population about which very little is known—the design will matter a lot less than the execution in the field. For participant observation studies, execution in the field will be almost everything, as a skilled and careful observer with ample time to devote to the project can identify something interesting, novel, and important from nearly any field site they observe. This diversity suggests that a discussion of how to assess proposals must be general, rather than dogmatic. To that end, we outline briefly what we would consider in evaluating a proposal on the basis of the indicators of quality discussed in this book.

Criteria and Proposals

EXPOSURE. The first and most important issue we would consider is exposure, the number of hours the researcher expects to spend either interviewing individuals or conducting observation. We have noted that exposure is the sine qua non, as without it most of the criteria we have discussed are impossible to attain. We must stress that, because of the diversity of approaches to fieldwork, we do not consider sample size as such to be an appropriate consideration. A handful of participants interviewed and observed over hundreds of hours has been the hallmark of many outstanding qualitative studies.[6] The core criterion here is time, and we believe that any evaluator of qualitative research would do well to replace the notion of sample size with that of exposure: the number of people with the number of hours. An effective study could examine many people for a few hours each or a few people for many hours each. The appropriate number of people, or of cases, would depend on the question. But regardless of the question, spending a lot of total time exposed to people or field sites will be indispensable.

Too short an exposure period would raise a red flag. Empirically strong interview studies with less than a hundred hours of exposure are not impossible but are uncommon, and they would require a narrow question and limited research aims. Strong participant observation studies often involve over a thousand hours of fieldwork, but a highly targeted study could accomplish its aims with far fewer.

PRELIMINARY DATA. Because the criteria we have described can only fully be detected in the data, we would consider the presence and quality of preliminary data. Most large-scale studies begin with preliminary work, and an effective proposal would use that work to demonstrate the quality of the data collected. Doing so would involve not merely reporting that progress has been made but in fact presenting the preliminary findings, thereby making evident the researcher's abilities. If the proposal did so, then the degree to which the researcher sought cognitive empathy would be clear, as well as some sense of sensitivity about heterogeneity. The data presented, if strong, would be palpable, even if limited. That is, several of the indicators we have discussed in this book would begin to show. In addition, preliminary data would inevitably uncover many issues that a newcomer to a site or population would not have known to address. Conversely, a proposal for a large-scale study that had not been preceded by any time in the field would signal trouble ahead; it would probably best be reconceived as a smaller, seed-funding proposal for that exploratory work.

RATIONALE. We would also consider rationale. We have shown that qualitative studies range widely in approach, and that researchers disagree vehemently on what is optimal. They even disagree on whether a formal design is appropriate. In this context, we would consider whether the proposal provided the rationale behind each element of the study *as the researcher has conceived it*. For example, if the researcher is proposing formal hypotheses, predetermined sample sizes, strict interview or observation protocols, and formal coding schemes, then the proposal, rather than assuming such decisions are self-evident, would justify each element of the approach—for example, that it is formalizing hypotheses because the literature has provided two clear and contradictory expectations, that it needs a strict interview protocol because many different interviewers will be involved, and so forth. If the researcher is, say, specifying a topic and field site but eschewing hypotheses and instead allowing the full research questions to emerge inductively from the field, then the proposal would explain the motivation behind each element of its approach—for example, that the literature is too new to generate convincing hypotheses, that the many unknown unknowns in the population require being responsive to discoveries in the field, and so forth.

An effective discussion of the rationale would include an acknowledgment of the limitations of each element of the approach and an explanation of why, in spite of those constraints, the element is still warranted. Every element of every approach—specifying or not specifying hypotheses, using strict or open interview or observation protocols, enrolling many or few participants, observing one or multiple field sites, coding inductively or deductively, and so forth—has well-understood strengths and limitations. We would look for a discussion of those limitations.

Thus, a red flag would be a proposal that merely asserted, rather than justified, its approach. Simply asserting that a study will be based on one hundred one-hour interviews without discussing both the motivation and the drawbacks would be as troublesome as simply stating that it will be based on "grounded theory" without defining what that means, explaining why it is needed, and being clear on the limitations—in both cases, the reader would have no basis to believe the author has considered major issues likely to affect the interpretation of the data. A proposal that is not explicit about the rationale for its approach could signal an unreflective researcher.

SELF-AWARENESS. We would also consider self-awareness, some elements of which can in fact be seen at the proposal stage. As we have noted, an effective researcher not only manages their influence on access, disclosure, and interpretation but also anticipates that influence. A strong proposal would consider the extent to which the researcher's identity—as we have used that term—affects, at a minimum, whom they can access and how much is disclosed. A researcher who has not considered such matters has not effectively reflected on the potential for weak or misconstrued data.

ANTICIPATED FOLLOW-UP. As we discussed in chapter 4, over the course of their fieldwork, qualitative researchers will inevitably encounter statements or events they did not anticipate and questions they cannot answer with the data they have on hand. The researcher's awareness of this fact and demonstrated willingness to act upon it are strong signals. A strong proposal is frank about the unknown and has, as appropriate, either a formal plan or at least an expectation that unknown discoveries will require a response.

In contrast, failure to anticipate following up can be detected in at least three red flags. One is the promise of a quick turnaround. A proposal that proposes a short delivery time in answer to a large question is signaling, in addition to limited exposure, either a decision to not follow up on the many issues that will necessarily emerge in the field or lack of knowledge that a lot of the discovery will require one or another form of follow-up. Another red flag is the presence of too many research questions. As the number of initial questions grows, the number of expected unknowns in a project grows exponentially, and the only way to address a large number of research questions within a reasonable time is by either failing to follow up or else addressing many of the questions poorly. A third, related red flag is either a questionnaire with a large number of formal questions or a field plan with a large number of either field sites or preset objects of observation. A detailed interview guide works very well in a survey but increasingly poorly as the interviews are more in-depth, since the latter require the ability to respond to statements not anticipated. A field plan with either many sites or many planned points of observation can only be resolved by dropping most foci once in the field, by extending the research project for years and even decades, or by failing to follow up while in the field. Qualitative projects inevitably grow. Failure to anticipate this fact is a sign of inexperience.

Our list of considerations is not exhaustive. It certainly excludes discussion of all the components necessary in any kind of research proposal, such as a clear question and an important or interesting topic. It also excludes all of the issues that must be evaluated that are particular to a given design, such as the quality of a sampling frame in a study that proposes statistical representativeness or the promise of true discovery in one that proposes grounded theorizing. But the issues we would consider, general in nature, would matter in most kinds of qualitative proposals we can think of. In the end, our hope is that those evaluating proposals, like those assessing finished works, adopt an approach consonant with what we have aimed to make a case for, one that is critical but not dogmatic, open-minded but thoughtful, cognizant of differences across methods but nonetheless concerned with signals of quality.

Notes

Preface

1. Small 2018. The uncertainty does not only reflect a lack of qualitative literacy. After all, seasoned ethnographers were among those who could not quite articulate how they distinguish sound from unsound work—even though it is clear that they have the capacity to do so. Part of the issue is that field-workers have rarely been expected to articulate—to list one by one—the criteria they are using. Among our aims is to start bringing such criteria explicitly to light.

2. For example, outlets such as the *New York Times*'s The Upshot regularly produce reports with actual data, in which readers can see where, say, their own school districts lie in a national distribution of achievement scores or their personal income places them in comparison to other Americans.

3. For example, all top ten programs in sociology require at least two courses in statistical methods, but only three require all PhD students to complete a standalone qualitative methods course. Berkeley, Princeton, Stanford, UCLA, and UNC all require a two-course stats sequence but do not require a standalone qualitative or fields methods course. Michigan and Chicago allow students to use a qualitative methods course to fulfill a methods elective requirement but do not require all students to take a stand-alone qualitative methods course; they do, however, require that students take two or more courses in statistical methods. Only Harvard, Northwestern, and Wisconsin require that all students take a stand-alone qualitative methods course; they all also require a two-course sequence in quantitative methods. The top-ten ranked programs were identified

using US News & World Report Rankings from 2021 and included UC Berkeley, Harvard, Princeton, Michigan, Stanford, UCLA, Chicago, UNC, and Wisconsin (see www.usnews.com/best-graduate-schools/top-humanities-schools/sociology-rankings). Graduates of top-ranked programs are disproportionately likely to hold faculty positions at top-ranked programs and disproportionately likely to hold faculty positions in PhD-granting institutions more generally (Clauset, Arbesman, and Larremore 2015; Fetner 2018). Faculty in top departments, in turn, disproportionately hold positions of influence in academia, including as journal editors and members of grant review panels.

Introduction

1. Hammersley 1992; Denzin 2010.

2. Maher and colleagues, for example, find that "Economists testify before the US Congress far more often than other social scientists, and constitute a larger proportion of the social scientists testifying in industry and government positions." See Maher et al. 2020. See also Hirschman and Berman 2014; Christensen 2020; Espeland and Stevens 2008.

3. The list of relevant research is far too long to adequately summarize. Yet scholars across various disciplines have offered review essays outlining the contributions of qualitative research. See, for example, Davies 2000; Nastasi and Schensul 2005; Riehl 2001; Newman and Massengill 2006; Alasuutari 2010; Doz 2011.

4. While astronomy and history as academic disciplines have been practiced for millennia, sociology, political science, economics, and psychology are but a few centuries old.

5. Bloor 2010; Sadovnik 2006; Hammersley 2000; Green and Britten 1998; Wedeen 2010; Gerring 2017.

6. See, for example, Small, Manduca, and Johnston 2018; Klinenberg 2018; Hagerman 2018; Hughes 2021; Lareau and Goyette 2014; Brown-Saracino 2017.

7. See, for example, Kajanus et al. 2019; Gansen 2017, 2018; Lewis 2003; Calarco 2018; Carter 2007; Morris 2018; Oeur 2018; Rios 2011; Shedd 2015; Jack 2019; Guhin 2020; Binder and Wood 2013; Tyson 2011; Lewis and Diamond 2015; Lewis-McCoy 2014; Murray et al. 2019; Posey-Maddox 2014; Cucchiara 2013; Morris 2005; Armstrong and Hamilton 2015.

8. See, for example, Menjívar 2011; Carrillo 2018; Durand and Massey 2004; Mckenzie and Menjívar 2011; Garcia 2019.

9. See, for example, Wingfield and Chavez 2020; Rivera 2016; Friedman and Laurison 2019; Chavez 2021.

10. See, for example, Collins 2019; Damaske 2011; Edin and Kefalas 2011; Edin and Lein 1997; Dow 2019; Gerson 1985; Swidler 2013; Hochschild 1989.

11. See, for example, Abrego 2006; Anderson 2009; Gonzales 2011; Rios 2011; Kwon 2014; Van Cleve 2016.

12. See, for example, Mazelis 2016; Pattillo 1999; Lareau 2011; Silva 2013; Wingfield 2009, 2010; Black 2010; Stack 1974; Lacy 2007; Ray 2017.

13. For example, Lareau's *Unequal Childhoods* and Hochschild's *The Second Shift* have each been cited more than ten thousand times, with many citations by quantitative studies of either inequality or time use. See Lareau 2011; Hochschild 1989.

14. Mario Small has testified before the Joint Economic Committee of the US Senate based on his work on social capital. See Small 2017b, 2009b. Tressie McMillan Cottom hast testified before the US Senate regarding the reauthorization of the Higher Education Act, based on her work on college education. See Cottom 2018, 2019. Cynthia Miller-Idriss has testified before the US House of Representatives on white nationalism, based on her work on domestic terrorism. See Miller-Idriss 2018, 2019. Sara Goldrick-Rab, author of *Paying the Price*, founded the Hope Center for College, Community, and Justice, which uses research to influence policy and practice in higher education. See Goldrick-Rab 2016. Stephanie De Luca's research on affordable housing has had a direct impact on several bipartisan legislative efforts. See https://otheramerica.org/policy-impact.

15. Johansson, Risberg, and Hamberg 2003; King, Keohane, and Verba 1994; Aspers and Corte 2019; Shuval et al. 2011; Aguinaldo 2004.

16. King, Keohane, and Verba 1994.

17. McKeown 1999; Hopf 2007; Kratochwil 2007.

18. Brady and Collier 2004; Moses and Knutsen 2019.

19. Ragin, Nagel, and White 2004:7.

20. Lamont and White 2005; Ragin, Nagel, and White 2004.

21. Ragin, Nagel, and White 2004:3-4.

22. Lamont and White 2005:4.

23. Ragin, Nagel, and White 2004:4 ("researcher's presence [and] biography"); Lamont and White 2005 ("explain case selection").

24. Becker 2009:9.

25. Cohen 2017.

26. Lubet 2017.

27. Clarke 2007; Levers 2013; Jerolmack and Khan 2014; Small 2015; Reyes 2018; Rios 2015; Jerolmack and Murphy 2019; Murphy et al. 2020; Katz 2019.

28. Henrich, Heine, and Norenzayan 2010.

29. Rubin 2017; Kerr 1998; Head et al 2015; Konnikova 2015; Simmons, Nelson, and Simonsohn 2011.

30. Resnick 2018, 2021.

31. Gauchat 2012; Resnik 2011; Anvari and Lakens 2018. The refusal by many Americans to wear masks amid hundreds of thousands of COVID-19 deaths is a stark example.

32. Gewin 2016; Wicherts et al. 2016; Nosek and Lindsay 2018. We note that there are many differences across disciplines, and not all practices work for all quantitative social science. Preregistering hypotheses, for example, is far more common in psychology than in other fields and would not necessarily improve the quality of research in much of data-driven social science, where inductive methods are common.

33. Khan 2019; Marcus 2020.

34. Research sites may of course be *revisited*, but revisits and replications are different things, and revisiting a site poses entirely different sets of questions. See Burawoy 2003.

35. Murphy et al. 2020.

36. Jerolmack and Murphy 2019; Reyes 2018.

37. Alexander et al. 2020; Mannheimer et al. 2019.

38. Murphy et al. 2020; Tsai et al. 2016; Krystalli 2018; McLeod and O'Connor 2021.

39. That the site was Boston's North End was not publicly known until many decades after the book's publication. See Whyte 1943.

40. Aspers and Corte 2019.

41. Small 2011.

42. Small 2011:60.

43. Small 2011:60.

44. Glaser and Strauss 1999 (grounded theorizing); Burawoy 1998 (extended case method).

45. Riessman 1990; Black 2010; Watkins-Hayes 2019 (biological narratives); Andrews et al. 2010; Edin and Lein 1997 (statistical regressions).

46. Anderson 1999; Duneier 1999; Lareau 2011 (classic ethnographies); Putnam 2001; Collins 2004; White, White, and Johansen 2005 (quantitative analyses).

47. While interviewers and participant observers can collect a broad array of data, including video clips, photographs, and newspaper clippings, the data we focus on are (audio) transcripts and field notes. These are the two most common types of data analyzed, respectively, by interviewers and ethnographers. Moreover, as we shall see throughout the book, covering more types of data would dramatically expand the issues we need to discuss. In addition, note that it is possible for researchers to analyze data, whether transcripts or field notes, that they did not collect. However, most of our discussion focuses on the analysis of self-collected data.

48. For discussions of these debates and perspectives, see Devault 1990; Fonow and Cook 1991; Gluck and Patai 1991; Hammersley 1992; Miles and Huberman 1994; Anderson and Jack 1997; Visweswaran 1997; Glaser and Strauss 1999; Foley 2002; Atkinson et al. 2007; Hammersley and Atkinson 1995; Duncan 2005; Nayak 2006; Wedeen 2010; Charmaz 2014; Chávez 2012; Maxwell 2013; Creswell and Poth 2016; Gluck and Patai 1991; Gerring 2017; Lareau and Shultz 2019; Davis and Craven 2020; Gerson and Damaske 2020; Lareau 2021.

49. Miles 1979; Miles and Huberman 1994.

50. Becker 2009; Tavory and Timmermans 2014; Katz 2015.

51. Knapik 2006; Pezalla, Pettigrew, and Miller-Day 2012; Xu and Storr 2012.

52. Driedger et al. 2006; Conlon et al., 2015; Mauthner and Doucet 2008.

53. May and Pattillo-McCoy 2000. To be clear, large research teams of interviewers and ethnographers can and do collect qualitative data as well. See, for example, Andrews et al. 2010; Lareau 2011; Creese and Blackledge 2012; Conlon et al. 2015; Jarzabkowski, Bednarek, and Cabantous 2015; Harris, Wojcik, and Allison 2020. In such contexts, one way PIs address the issue is to formalize the questionnaires, ensure everyone asks the same question in the same order, and practice follow-up questioning to ensure every researcher

follows the same approach. These projects function essentially as surveys with preset but open-ended questions. At the other extreme, PIs may let a thousand flowers bloom, training researchers in the craft of interviewing but allowing them to probe interviews where they go. Others mix approaches, requiring a set of questions to start every interview that are consistent for all respondents (a portion that is essentially a survey) and then shifting to a set of questions that lead to more open, interactive, inductively pursued conversations (a portion that is a standard in-depth interview).

54. We set aside deeper epistemological questions about whether any researcher collecting data through any method is ever not part of the data, and whether a strict distinction between objectivity and subjectivity in the data collection process can ever be achieved. There is no doubt that reactivity is greater in an open-ended interview than in a survey. There is no doubt that reactivity is greater in traditional participant observation than in other methods.

55. King, Keohane, and Verba 1994. But see Mahoney 2000, 2007.

56. Shaw 1930; Whyte 1943; Fenno 1966; Liebow 1967; Stack 1974; Kanter 1977; Willis 1977; Anderson 1978; MacLeod 1987; Perry 1994; Duneier 1999; Pattillo 1999; Anderson 1999; Small 2004; Desmond 2008; Lareau 2011; Armstrong and Hamilton 2015; Gillespie 2013; Van Cleve 2016.

57. See, e.g., Small 2009a.

58. To be sure, some of the questions one worries about in qualitative field studies may bear some analogy to some of these concepts, and we make note of when they do. But as we will show, these worries are motivated by entirely different questions.

59. See, for example, Emerson, Fretz, and Shaw 2011; Gerson and Damaske 2020; Weiss 1995; Denzin and Lincoln 2011; Hollstein 2011; Lareau 2021; Creswell and Poth 2016.

60. Duneier 1999; Lareau 2011; Calarco 2018.

61. Small 2009b, 2017a; Lareau 2000; Hochschild 1989, 2016.

Chapter 1. Cognitive Empathy

1. See Small 2017a.
2. See Small 2017a. See also Becker 1967; Fine 1993.
3. See, for example, Simi et al. 2017; Bedera 2021.

4. Smith 1822: 2.

5. Mead 1934.

6. Mead 1934:125.

7. Mead 1934:155.

8. Hausheer 1996.

9. Dilthey 1927:123.

10. Dilthey 1927:123.

11. Weber 1978:4.

12. Saiedi 1992.

13. Geertz 1973:5.

14. Edin and Kefalas 2011.

15. Weber 1978:11, also 8–9.

16. Mills 1940; Scott and Lyman 1968; Czarniawska 2004; Benzecry 2011; Damaske 2011, 2013; Fridman 2016; Lizardo 2021; Vaisey 2009.

17. Small and Cook 2021; Deutscher, Pestello, and Pestello 1993.

18. Freese and Kevern 2013.

19. Small 2015.

20. Small 2009b.

21. Small and Cook 2021; Deutscher, Pestello, and Pestello 1993; Pugh 2013; Gerson and Damaske 2020.

22. There are many published books and journal articles that we could have selected as examples to include in this book. In the interest of brevity, we include two in each chapter—one illustrating the indicator as it appears in interview-based research and one as it appears in ethnographic work.

23. Watkins-Hayes 2019. *Remaking a Life* focuses primarily on black women living with HIV; however, some respondents are not black, including Trisha, who is white, and Rosaria, who is Latina.

24. Small 2015.

25. Watkins-Hayes 2019:1.

26. Watkins-Hayes 2019:4.

27. Watkins-Hayes 2019:5.

28. Lareau 2021; Devault 1990; Anderson and Jack 1997.

29. Geertz 1973.

30. Emerson, Fretz, and Shaw 2011.

31. Pugh 2013; Small and Cook 2021.

32. Deener 2012.

33. Deener 2012:xiii.

34. Deener 2012:44.

35. Deener 2012:45.

36. Deener 2012:45.

37. Deener 2012:45.

38. Deener 2012:45–46.

39. Deener 2012:46.

Chapter 2. Heterogeneity

1. Ackerman et al. 2006.

2. Hochschild 2016.

3. Ackerman et al. 2006.

4. Quattrone and Jones 1980; Cikara, Bruneau, and Saxe 2011; Linville, Fischer, and Salovey 1989; Messick and Mackie 1989; Park, Judd, and Ryan 1991; Zhou et al. 2020; Reggev et al. 2019; Simon and Pettigrew 1990.

5. Van Bavel, Packer, and Cunningham 2008.

6. Merton 1972.

7. See, for example, Kanter 1977; Willis 1977; Bosk 1979; Fine 1987; Pattillo 1993; Lewis 2003; Pascoe 2011; Tyson 2011; Khan 2012; Lewis and Diamond 2015; Mueller and Abrutyn 2016.

8. This happens, too, among researchers who study their own ethnic, class, gender, or other group, unless the setting is the one in which the researcher grew up, such that the researcher, not an outgroup member, already had a strong heterogeneous understanding. See, for example, Desmond 2008; Khan 2012.

9. Abrego 2006; Gonzales 2011; Garcia 2019.

10. Hochschild 2016.

11. Stuart 2020.

12. Stuart 2016; Avery 2012.

13. Lareau 2011; Desmond 2017.

14. MacLeod 1987.

15. Small 2004.

16. Pattillo 1999; Jones 2018; Watkins-Hayes 2019.

17. Shaw 1930.

18. Whyte 1943; Stack 1974.

19. Small and Cook 2021.

20. Schwartz 2000; McFarland 1981; Moore 2002; Pustejovsky and Spillane 2009; Jensen, Watanabe, and Richters 1999; Vitale, Armenakis, and Field 2008.

21. For examples of the various approaches, see Bonilla-Silva 2003; Carter 2007; Small 2017a; Small 2009b; Calarco et al. 2021; Calarco and Anderson 2021.

22. Hughes 2021.

23. Hughes 2021:10.

24. Hughes 2021:10.

25. Hughes 2021:10.

26. Hughes 2021:10.

27. Hughes 2021:14.

28. Small 2015.

29. Raudenbush 2020.

30. Raudenbush 2020:20.

31. Raudenbush 2020:20.

32. Raudenbush 2020:20.

33. Raudenbush 2020:20.

34. Raudenbush 2020:21.

35. Raudenbush 2020:31.

36. Raudenbush 2020:29.

37. Raudenbush 2020:33 ("highly integrated"); 34–35 (access to formal health care).

38. Raudenbush 2020:25.

Chapter 3. Palpability

1. Simmel 1909; Whitehead 1925; Merton 1973; Toscano 2008; Tavory and Timmermans 2014.

2. Simmel 1909; Merton 1973; Hodgson 2001.

3. This is an ontological realist position, which we take to be essential for empirical social science.

4. It should be clear that palpability is not transparency; the specific people or places described in the research need not be named. Effective fieldworkers provide enough concrete data about the specific people, places, and

events that they are interpretable regardless of whether the researcher decided to name them.

5. King, Keohane, and Verba 1994.

6. Weiss 1995; Small 2017a; Gerson and Damaske 2020.

7. Weiss 1995; Gerson and Damaske 2020; Lareau 2021.

8. Lee and Zhou 2015.

9. Lee and Zhou 2015:53.

10. Lee and Zhou 2015:54–55.

11. Thorne 1999.

12. Thorne 1999:76.

13. Thorne 1999:76.

Chapter 4. Follow-Up

1. Knapik 2006; Pezalla, Pettigrew, and Miller-Day 2012; Xu and Storr 2012.

2. May and Pattillo-McCoy 2000.

3. For example, Krause 2014.

4. See Small 2009a.

5. See Small 2011; Rinaldo and Guhin 2019 (other types of data). See, for example, Bonilla-Silva 2003; Carter 2007; Small 2017a; Friedman and Laurison 2019; Calarco and Anderson 2021 (large-scale surveys). See, for example, Pascoe 2011; Khan 2012; Rivera 2016 (ethnographic observations).

6. For example, see Small 2017a.

7. For several examples, see Rinaldo and Guhin 2019.

8. Small 2011.

9. Glaser and Strauss 1999; Small 2009a; Charmaz 2014.

10. Glaser and Strauss 1999; Guest, Bunce, and Johnson 2006; Charmaz 2014; Fusch and Ness 2015; Hennink, Kaiser, and Marconi 2017; Weller et al. 2018; Small 2017b.

11. Depending on the context, the number can be as few as a dozen. For studies on how many interviews are required for saturation, see Guest, Bunce, and Johnson 2006; Hennink, Kaiser, and Marconi 2017; Weller et al. 2018.

12. Takacs 2020.

13. Takacs 2020:260.

14. Takacs 2020:260.

15. Takacs 2020:260.

16. Takacs 2020:258.

17. And even one who did so—who, as a kind of field experiment, say, sat still on a bench in a park for hours on end and only recorded what they observed—would produce fieldnotes consisting of endless lists of unconfirmed first impressions. There are traditions in which this kind of observation is used to passively collect quantitative data on a predetermined set of events. This tradition was common, for example, in psychology in the middle of the twentieth century. That tradition would not produce qualitative fieldnotes of the kind that are the focus of this book.

18. See, for example, Burawoy 1998; Glaser and Strauss 1999; Simmons and Smith 2019; Pacheco-Vega 2020.

19. Small 2011.

20. Vaughan 2004; Small 2004; Twine 2006; Ho 2009; Cucchiara 2013; Shedd 2015; Vargas 2016; Ewing 2018; Calarco 2020; Matthews 2022; Stuber 2021 (contextualized ethnography); Rinaldo and Guhin 1999; Van Cleve 2016; Calarco 2018; Hagerman 2018; McKenna 2019; Güran 2020 (interview-ethnographic study).

21. Soss 1999; Small 2009b; Desmond 2017; Calarco and Anderson 2021 (statistical representativeness); McKenna 2019; Rafalow 2020; Güran 2020 (online interactions).

22. Brown-Saracino 2017.

23. Brown-Saracino 2017:254.

24. Brown-Saracino 2017:258.

25. Brown-Saracino 2017:258.

26. Brown-Saracino 2017:258–59.

27. Brown-Saracino 2017:259.

28. Brown-Saracino 2017:259.

29. Brown-Saracino 2017:257.

Chapter 5. Self-Awareness

1. Heisenberg 1977.

2. Landsberger 1958.

3. Fine 1993; Labaree 2002; Fox 2004; Monahan and Fisher 2010; Trnka and Lorencova 2016; Paradis and Sutkin 2017; West and Blom 2017.

4. Freeman and Butler 1976; Reese et al. 1986; Dionne 2014.

5. Dommeyer et al. 2009.

6. Kane and Macaulay 1993; Davis et al. 2010; Adida et al. 2016; White et al. 2018.

7. Cotter, Cohen, and Coulter 1982; Hatchett and Schuman 1975; Davis 1997; An and Winship 2017; White et al. 2005. Experimental research has also found higher scores by women and African Americans on tests when the latter are administered by experimenters of their same gender or race. See Marx and Roman 2002; Marx and Goff 2005.

8. Benstead 2014; Blaydes and Gillum 2013.

9. Moskos 2009; Armenta 2016.

10. Riessman 1990; Fonow and Cook 1991; Fine 1993; Beoku-Betts 1994; Coffey 1999; de Andrade 2000; Berger 2015; Hoang 2015; Krause 2014.

11. See, for example, Devault 1990; Burawoy 1991, 2003; Bourdieu and Wacquant 1992; Davies 1998; Collins 2000; Foley 2002; Venkatesh 2013; Small 2015; Lichterman 2017.

12. Humphreys 2005; Anderson 2006; Delamont 2009; Adams and Holman Jones 2011.

13. Peabody et al. 1990; Khan 2012; Mears 2020; Stuber 2021.

14. Simi et al. 2017; Hammersley and Atkinson 1995; Merton 1972; Venkatesh 2009.

15. Merton 1972; de Andrade 2000; Labaree 2002; Hodkinson 2005; Ergun and Erdemir 2010; Hoang 2015.

16. Sixsmith, Boneham, and Goldring 2003; Taylor 2011; Bucerius 2013; Greene 2014.

17. Goffman 1956, 1959; Riessman 1987; Edwards 1990; Hoang 2015; Small and Cook 2021.

18. Glaser and Strauss 1999.

19. Burawoy 1991:4.

20. See, for example, Brown 2017.

21. Vatican 1993.

22. See, for example, Deutscher, Pestello, and Pestello 1993; Small and Cook 2021; Dean and Whyte 1958; Schwartz 2000.

23. Riessman 1987; Beoku-Betts 1994; Gibson and Abrams 2003.

24. Small 2017a; Cotter, Cohen, and Coulter 1982; Hatchett and Schuman 1975; Davis 1997; An and Winship 2017; White et al. 2018; Song and Parker 1995; Gibson and Abrams 2003; Dionne 2014; Adida et al. 2016.

25. Merton 1972; Labaree 2002; Taylor 2011; Blee 2019.

26. Ephesians 5:21–32. See also US Conference of Catholic Bishops 2021.

27. Brown 2018.

28. Brown 2018:6.

29. Brown 2018:6.

30. Brown 2018:195.

31. Brown 2018:195.

32. Stack 1974.

33. Stack 1974:ix.

34. Stack 1974:ix.

35. Stack 1974:x.

36. Stack 1974:xi.

37. Stack 1974:10.

Conclusion

1. See, for example, Dworkin 2012.

2. See, for example, Simmons and Smith 2019.

Appendix: A Note on Proposals

1. In contrast, a "series" of experiments often is, as the findings in one experiment inform the design of the next.

2. See, for example, Whyte 1943; Stack 1974; Duneier 1999.

3. Becker 2009. See also Ragin, Nagel, and White 2004; Lamont and White 2005.

4. Becker 2009:548.

5. Becker 2009:547. We must note that many qualitative researchers, particularly in-depth interviewers, have been successful with projects that were extensively research designed before execution. For projects of this kind, we believe many of the points in the two NSF guidelines will prove apt.

But many projects do not work this way at all, and evaluating them on the basis of the wrong criteria undermines good science. Indeed, by some such criteria, the majority of the best ethnographies in US history would not have been funded.

6. See, for example, MacLeod 1987; Lareau 2011; Ray 2017; Willis 1977.

References

Abrego, Leisy Janet. 2006. "'I Can't Go to College Because I Don't Have Papers': Incorporation Patterns of Latino Undocumented Youth." *Latino Studies* 4(3):212–31. https://doi.org/10.1057/palgrave.lst.8600200.

Ackerman, Joshua M., Jenessa R. Shapiro, Steven L. Neuberg, Douglas T. Kenrick, D. Vaughn Becker, Vladas Griskevicius, Jon K. Maner, and Mark Schaller. 2006. "They All Look the Same to Me (Unless They're Angry): From Out-Group Homogeneity to Out-Group Heterogeneity." *Psychological Science* 17(10):836–40. https://doi.org/10.1111/j.1467-9280.2006 .01790.x.

Adams, Tony E., and Stacy Holman Jones. 2011. "Telling Stories: Reflexivity, Queer Theory, and Autoethnography." *Cultural Studies ↔ Critical Methodologies* 11(2):108–16. https://doi-org/10.1177/1532708611401329.

Adida, Claire L., Karen E. Ferree, Daniel N. Posner, and Amanda Lea Robinson. 2016. "Who's Asking? Interviewer Coethnicity Effects in African Survey Data." *Comparative Political Studies* 49(12):1630–60. https://doi .org/10.1177/0010414016633487.

Aguinaldo, Jeffrey P. 2004. "Rethinking Validity in Qualitative Research from a Social Constructionist Perspective: Fro." *Qualitative Report* 9(1):127–36.

Alasuutari, Pertti. 2010. "The Rise and Relevance of Qualitative Research." *International Journal of Social Research Methodology* 13(2):139–55. https:// doi.org/10.1080/13645570902966056.

Alexander, Steven M., Kristal Jones, Nathan J. Bennett, Amber Budden, Michael Cox, Mercè Crosas, Edward T. Game, Janis Geary, R. Dean

Hardy, Jay T. Johnson, Sebastian Karcher, Nicole Motzer, Jeremy Pittman, Heather Randell, Julie A. Silva, Patricia Pinto da Silva, Carly Strasser, Colleen Strawhacker, Andrew Stuhl, and Nic Weber. 2020. "Qualitative Data Sharing and Synthesis for Sustainability Science." *Nature Sustainability* 3(2):81–88. https://doi.org/10.1038/s41893-019-0434-8.

An, Weihua, and Christopher Winship. 2017. "Causal Inference in Panel Data with Application to Estimating Race-of-Interviewer Effects in the General Social Survey." *Sociological Methods & Research* 46(1):68–102. https://doi.org/10.1177/0049124115600614.

Anderson, Elijah. 1978. *A Place on the Corner*. Chicago: University of Chicago Press.

———. 1999. *Code of the Street: Decency, Violence, and the Moral Life of the Inner City*. New York: W. W. Norton.

———. 2009. *Against the Wall: Poor, Young, Black, and Male*. Philadelphia: University of Pennsylvania Press.

Anderson, Kathryn, and Dana C. Jack. 1997. *Learning to Listen: Interview Techniques and Analyses*. New York: Routledge.

Anderson, Leon. 2006. "Analytic Autoethnography." *Journal of Contemporary Ethnography* 35(4):373–95. https://doi-org/10.1177/0891241605280449.

Andrews, Kenneth T., Marshall Ganz, Matthew Baggetta, Hahrie Han, and Chaeyoon Lim. 2010. "Leadership, Membership, and Voice: Civic Associations That Work." *American Journal of Sociology* 115(4):1191–1242. https://doi.org/10.1086/649060.

Anvari, Farid, and Daniël Lakens. 2018. "The Replicability Crisis and Public Trust in Psychological Science." *Comprehensive Results in Social Psychology* 3(3):266–86. https://doi.org/10.1080/23743603.2019.1684822.

Armenta, Amada. 2016. "Between Public Service and Social Control: Policing Dilemmas in the Era of Immigration Enforcement." *Social Problems* 63(1):111–26. https://doi.org/10.1093/socpro/spv024.

Armstrong, Elizabeth A., and Laura T. Hamilton. 2015. *Paying for the Party: How College Maintains Inequality*. Reissue ed. Cambridge, MA: Harvard University Press.

Aspers, Patrik, and Ugo Corte. 2019. "What Is Qualitative in Qualitative Research." *Qualitative Sociology* 42(2):139–60. https://doi.org/10.1007/s11133-019-9413-7.

Atkinson, Paul, Sara Delamont, Amanda Coffey, John Lofland, and Lyn Lofland. 2007. *Handbook of Ethnography*. Thousand Oaks, CA: Sage.

Avery, Jacob. 2012. "Down and Out in Atlantic City." *ANNALS of the American Academy of Political and Social Science* 642(1):139–51. https://doi.org/10.1177/0002716212438196.

Becker, Howard S. 1967. "Whose Side Are We On?" *Social Problems* 14(3):239–47. https://doi.org/10.2307/799147.

———. 2009. "How to Find Out How to Do Qualitative Research." *International Journal of Communication* 3(0):9.

Bedera, Nicole. 2021. "Moaning and Eye Contact: Men's Use of Ambiguous Signals in Attributions of Consent to Their Partners." *Violence against Women* 27(15-16) https://doi.org/10.1177/1077801221992870.

Benstead, Lindsay J. 2014. "Does Interviewer Religious Dress Affect Survey Responses? Evidence from Morocco." *Politics & Religion* 7(4):734–60. http://dx.doi.org.proxyiub.uits.iu.edu/10.1017/S1755048314000455.

Benzecry, Claudio E. 2011. *The Opera Fanatic: Ethnography of an Obsession*. 1st ed. Chicago: University of Chicago Press.

Beoku-Betts, Josephine. 1994. "When Black Is Not Enough: Doing Field Research among Gullah Women." *NWSA Journal* 6(3):413–33.

Berger, Roni. 2015. "Now I See It, Now I Don't: Researcher's Position and Reflexivity in Qualitative Research." *Qualitative Research* 15(2):219–34. https://doi.org/10.1177/1468794112468475.

Binder, Amy J., and Kate Wood. 2013. *Becoming Right: How Campuses Shape Young Conservatives*. 1st ed. Princeton, NJ: Oxford University Press.

Black, Timothy. 2010. *When a Heart Turns Rock Solid: The Lives of Three Puerto Rican Brothers On and Off the Streets*. New York: Penguin.

Blaydes, Lisa, and Rachel M. Gillum. 2013. "Religiosity-of-Interviewer Effects: Assessing the Impact of Veiled Enumerators on Survey Response in Egypt." *Politics & Religion* 6(3):459–82. http://dx.doi.org.proxyiub.uits.iu.edu/10.1017/S1755048312000557.

Blee, Kathleen. 2019. "How Field Relationships Shape Theorizing." *Sociological Methods & Research* 48(4):739–62. https://doi.org/10.1177/0049124117701482.

Bloor, Michael. 2010. "Addressing Social Problems through Qualitative Research." In *Qualitative Research*, edited by D. Silverman, 15-30. Thousand Oaks, CA: Sage.

Bonilla-Silva, Eduardo. 2003. *Racism without Racists: Color-Blind Racism and the Persistence of Racial Inequality in America*. Lanham, MD: Rowman & Littlefield.

Bosk, Charles L. 1979. *Forgive and Remember: Managing Medical Failure*. Chicago: University of Chicago Press.

Bourdieu, Pierre, and Loïc J. D. Wacquant. 1992. *An Invitation to Reflexive Sociology*. Chicago: University of Chicago Press.

Brady, Henry E., and David Collier. 2004. *Rethinking Social Inquiry: Diverse Tools, Shared Standards*. Lanham, MD: Rowman & Littlefield.

Brown, Dwane. 2017. "How One Man Convinced 200 Ku Klux Klan Members to Give Up Their Robes." NPR. August 20. www.npr.org/2017/08/20 /544861933/how-one-man-convinced-200-ku-klux-klan-members-to -give-up-their-robes.

Brown, Karida L. 2018. *Gone Home: Race and Roots through Appalachia*. Chapel Hill: University of North Carolina Press.

Brown-Saracino, Japonica. 2017. *How Places Make Us: Novel LBQ Identities in Four Small Cities*. Chicago: University of Chicago Press.

Bucerius, Sandra Meike. 2013. "Becoming a 'Trusted Outsider': Gender, Ethnicity, and Inequality in Ethnographic Research." *Journal of Contemporary Ethnography* 42(6):690–721. https://doi.org/10.1177/0891241 613497747.

Burawoy, Michael. 1991. "Reconstructing Social Theories." In *Ethnography Unbound*, edited by Michael Burawoy et al., 8–28. Chicago: University of California Press.

———. 1998. "The Extended Case Method." *Sociological Theory* 16(1):4–33. https://doi.org/10.1111/0735-2751.00040.

———. 2003. "Revisits: An Outline of a Theory of Reflexive Ethnography." *American Sociological Review* 68(5):645–79. https://doi.org/10.2307 /1519757.

Calarco, Jessica McCrory. 2018. *Negotiating Opportunities: How the Middle Class Secures Advantages in School*. New York: Oxford University Press.

———. 2020. "Avoiding Us versus Them: How Schools' Dependence on Privileged 'Helicopter' Parents Influences Enforcement of Rules." *American Sociological Review* 85(2):223–46. https://doi.org/10.1177 /0003122420905793.

Calarco, Jessica McCrory, and Elizabeth M. Anderson. 2021. "'I'm Not Gonna Put That on My Kids': Gendered Opposition to New Public Health Initiatives." *SocArxiv Papers*. https://doi.org/10.31235/osf.io/tv8zw.

Calarco, Jessica McCrory, Emily Meanwell, Elizabeth Anderson, and Amelia Knopf. 2021. "By Default: The Origins of Gendered Inequalities in Pandemic Parenting." *Socius* 7. https://doi.org/10.1177/2378023121 1038783.

Carrillo, Héctor. 2018. *Pathways of Desire: The Sexual Migration of Mexican Gay Men*. Chicago: University of Chicago Press.

Carter, Prudence L. 2007. *Keepin' It Real: School Success Beyond Black and White*. Illustrated ed. Oxford: Oxford University Press.

Charmaz, Kathy. 2014. *Constructing Grounded Theory*. 2nd ed. Thousand Oaks, CA: Sage.

Chavez, Koji. 2021. "Penalized for Personality: A Case Study of Asian-Origin Disadvantage at the Point of Hire." *Sociology of Race and Ethnicity* 7(2):226–46. https://doi.org/10.1177/2332649220922270.

Chávez, Minerva S. 2012. "Autoethnography, a Chicana's Methodological Research Tool: The Role of Storytelling for Those Who Have No Choice but to Do Critical Race Theory." *Equity & Excellence in Education* 45(2):334–48. https://doi.org/10.1080/10665684.2012.669196.

Christensen, Johan. 2020. *The Power of Economists within the State*. Stanford, CA: Stanford University Press.

Cikara, Mina, Emile G. Bruneau, and Rebecca R. Saxe. 2011. "Us and Them: Intergroup Failures of Empathy." *Current Directions in Psychological Science* 20(3):149–53. https://doi.org/10.1177/0963721411408713.

Clarke, Adele E. 2007. "Grounded Theory: Critiques, Debates, and Situational Analysis." In *The SAGE Handbook of Social Science Methodology*, 423–42. London: Sage.

Clauset, Aaron, Samuel Arbesman, and Daniel B. Larremore. 2015. "Systematic Inequality and Hierarchy in Faculty Hiring Networks," *Science Advances* 1(1). https://doi.org/10.1126/sciadv.1400005.

Coffey, Amanda. 1999. *The Ethnographic Self: Fieldwork and the Representation of Identity*. Thousand Oaks, CA: Sage.

Cohen, Philip N. 2017. "On the Run: Fugitive Life in an American City." *Social Forces* 95(4):e5–e5. https://doi.org/10.1093/sf/sov113.

Collins, Caitlyn. 2019. *Making Motherhood Work: How Women Manage Careers and Caregiving*. Princeton, NJ: Princeton University Press.

Collins, Patricia Hill. 2000. *Black Feminist Thought: Knowledge, Consciousness, and the Politics of Empowerment*. New York: Routledge.

Collins, Randall. 2004. "Rituals of Solidarity and Security in the Wake of Terrorist Attack." *Sociological Theory* 22(1):53–87. https://doi.org/10.1111/j .1467-9558.2004.00204.x.

Conlon, Catherine, Gemma Carney, Virpi Timonen, and Thomas Scharf. 2015. "'Emergent Reconstruction' in Grounded Theory: Learning from Team-Based Interview Research." *Qualitative Research* 15(1):39–56. https://doi.org/10.1177/1468794113495038.

Cotter, Patrick R., Jeffrey Cohen, and Philip B. Coulter. 1982. "Race-of-Interviewer Effects in Telephone Interviews." *Public Opinion Quarterly* 46(2):278–84.

Cottom, Tressie McMillan. 2018. *Lower Ed: The Troubling Rise of For-Profit Colleges in the New Economy*. New York: The New Press.

———. 2019. "Testimony of Dr. Tressie McMillan Cottom Regarding Reauthorizing the Higher Education Act: Strengthening Accountability to Protect Students and Taxpayers." U.S. Senate Committee on Health, Education, Labor & Pensions, April, Washington, DC.

Creese, Angela, and Adrian Blackledge. 2012. "Voice and Meaning-Making in Team Ethnography." *Anthropology & Education Quarterly* 43(3):306–24. https://doi.org/10.1111/j.1548-1492.2012.01182.x.

Creswell, John W., and Cheryl N. Poth. 2016. *Qualitative Inquiry and Research Design: Choosing Among Five Approaches*. Thousand Oaks, CA: Sage.

Cucchiara, Maia Bloomfield. 2013. *Marketing Schools, Marketing Cities*. Chicago: University of Chicago Press.

Czarniawska, Barbara. 2004. *Narratives in Social Science Research*. Thousand Oaks, CA: Sage.

Damaske, Sarah. 2011. *For the Family? How Class and Gender Shape Women's Work*. Illustrated ed. New York: Oxford University Press.

———. 2013. "Work, Family, and Accounts of Mothers' Lives Using Discourse to Navigate Intensive Mothering Ideals." *Sociology Compass* 7(6):436–44. https://doi.org/10.1111/soc4.12043.

Davies, Charlotte Aull. 1998. *Reflexive Ethnography: A Guide to Researching Selves and Others*. London: Routledge.

Davies, Philip. 2000. "Contributions from Qualitative Research." In *What Works? Evidence-Based Policy and Practice in Public Services*, edited by D. T. O. Huw and N. M Sandra.

Davis, Dána-Ain, and Christa Craven. 2020. "Feminist Ethnography." In *Companion to Feminist Studies*, edited by Nancy A. Naples, 281–99. Hoboken, NJ: John Wiley & Sons.

Davis, Darren W. 1997. "The Direction of Race of Interviewer Effects among African-Americans: Donning the Black Mask." *American Journal of Political Science* 41(1):309–22. https://doi.org/10.2307/2111718.

Davis, R. E., M. P. Couper, N. K. Janz, C. H. Caldwell, and K. Resnicow. 2010. "Interviewer Effects in Public Health Surveys." *Health Education Research* 25(1):14–26. https://doi.org/10.1093/her/cyp046.

de Andrade, Leila Lomba. 2000. "Negotiating from the Inside: Constructing Racial and Ethnic Identity in Qualitative Research." *Journal of Contemporary Ethnography* 29(3):268–90. https://doi.org/10.1177/089124100129023918.

Dean, John P., and William Foote Whyte. 1958. "How Do You Know If the Informant Is Telling the Truth?" *Human Organization* 17(2):34–38.

Deener, Andrew. 2012. *Venice: A Contested Bohemia in Los Angeles*. Illustrated ed. Chicago: University of Chicago Press.

Delamont, Sara. 2009. "The Only Honest Thing: Autoethnography, Reflexivity and Small Crises in Fieldwork." *Ethnography and Education* 4(1):51–63. https://doi-org/10.1080/17457820802703507.

Denzin, Norman K. 2010. "Moments, Mixed Methods, and Paradigm Dialogs." *Qualitative Inquiry* 16(6):419–27. https://doi.org/10.1177/1077800410364608.

Denzin, Norman K., and Yvonna S. Lincoln, eds. 2011. *The SAGE Handbook of Qualitative Research*. 4th ed. Thousand Oaks, CA: Sage.

Desmond, Matthew. 2008. *On the Fireline: Living and Dying with Wildland Firefighters*. Chicago: University of Chicago Press.

———. 2017. *Evicted: Poverty and Profit in the American City*. Reprint ed. New York: Broadway Books.

Deutscher, Irwin, Fred P. Pestello, and H. Frances G. Pestello. 1993. *Sentiments and Acts*. Piscataway, NJ: Transaction Publishers.

Devault, Marjorie L. 1990. "Talking and Listening from Women's Standpoint: Feminist Strategies for Interviewing and Analysis." *Social Problems* 37(1):96–116. https://doi.org/10.2307/800797.

Dilthey, Wilhelm. 1927. "The Understanding of Other Persons and Their Expressions of Life." In *Descriptive Psychology and Historical Understanding*, edited by W. Dilthey, 121–44. Dordrecht: Springer Netherlands.

Dionne, Kim Yi. 2014. "The Politics of Local Research Production: Surveying in a Context of Ethnic Competition." *Politics, Groups, and Identities* 2(3):459–80. https://doi.org/10.1080/21565503.2014.930691.

Dommeyer, Curt J., Elizabeth A. Lugo, J. D. Power, Kelly R. Riddle, and Lily Valdivia. 2009. "Using a White Lab Coat to Enhance the Response Rate to Personally Initiated, Self-Administered Surveys." *Journal of Applied Business and Economics* 9(2):67–76.

Dow, Dawn Marie. 2019. *Mothering While Black*. Oakland: University of California Press.

Doz, Yves. 2011. "Qualitative Research for International Business." *Journal of International Business Studies* 42(5):582–90. https://doi.org/10.1057/jibs.2011.18.

Driedger, S. Michelle, Cindy Gallois, Carrie B. Sanders, and Santesso Nancy. 2006. "Finding Common Ground in Team-Based Qualitative Research Using the Convergent Interviewing Method." *Qualitative Health Research* 16(8):1145–57. https://doi.org/10.1177/1049732306289705.

Duncan, Garrett Albert. 2005. "Critical Race Ethnography in Education: Narrative, Inequality and the Problem of Epistemology." *Race Ethnicity and Education* 8(1):93–114. https://doi.org/10.1080/1361332052000341015.

Duneier, Mitchell. 1999. *Sidewalk*. New York: Farrar, Straus and Giroux.

Durand, Jorge, and Douglas S. Massey. 2004. *Crossing the Border: Research from the Mexican Migration Project*. New York: Russell Sage Foundation.

Dworkin, Shari L. 2012. "Sample Size Policy for Qualitative Studies Using In-Depth Interviews." *Archives of Sexual Behavior* 41(6):1319–20. https://doi.org/10.1007/s10508-012-0016-6.

Edin, Kathryn, and Maria J. Kefalas. 2011. *Promises I Can Keep: Why Poor Women Put Motherhood before Marriage*. Berkeley: University of California Press.

Edin, Kathryn, and Laura Lein. 1997. *Making Ends Meet: How Single Mothers Survive Welfare and Low-Wage Work*. New York: Russell Sage Foundation.

Edwards, Rosalind. 1990. "Connecting Method and Epistemology: A White Women Interviewing Black Women." *Women's Studies International Forum* 13(5):477–90. https://doi.org/10.1016/0277-5395(90)90100-C.

Emerson, Robert M., Rachel I. Fretz, and Linda L. Shaw. 2011. *Writing Ethnographic Fieldnotes*. 2nd ed. Chicago: University of Chicago Press.

Ergun, Ayça, and Aykan Erdemir. 2010. "Negotiating Insider and Outsider Identities in the Field: 'Insider' in a Foreign Land; 'Outsider' in One's Own Land." *Field Methods* 22(1):16-38. https://doi.org/10.1177/1525822X 09349919.

Espeland, Wendy Nelson, and Mitchell L. Stevens. 2008. "A Sociology of Quantification." *European Journal of Sociology* 49(3):401-36.

Ewing, Eve L. 2018. *Ghosts in the Schoolyard: Racism and School Closings on Chicago's South Side*. 1st ed. Chicago: University of Chicago Press.

Fenno, Richard F. 1966. *The Power of the Purse: Appropriations Politics in Congress*. Boston: Little, Brown.

Fetner, Tina. 2018. "Who Hires Whom?" *Scatterplot* (blog). January 8. https://scatter.wordpress.com/2018/01/08/who-hires-whom/.

Fine, Gary Alan. 1987. *With the Boys: Little League Baseball and Preadolescent Culture*. Chicago: University of Chicago Press.

———. 1993. "Ten Lies of Ethnography: Moral Dilemmas of Field Research." *Journal of Contemporary Ethnography* 22(3):267-94. https://doi.org/10.1177 /089124193022003001.

Foley, Douglas E. 2002. "Critical Ethnography: The Reflexive Turn." *International Journal of Qualitative Studies in Education* 15(4):469-90. https://doi .org/10.1080/09518390210145534.

Fonow, Mary Margaret, and Judith A. Cook. 1991. *Beyond Methodology: Feminist Scholarship as Lived Research*. Bloomington: Indiana University Press.

Fox, Renée C. 2004. "Observations and Reflections of a Perpetual Fieldworker." *ANNALS of the American Academy of Political and Social Science* 595(1):309-26. https://doi.org/10.1177/0002716204266635.

Freeman, John, and Edgar W. Butler. 1976. "Some Sources of Interviewer Variance in Surveys." *Public Opinion Quarterly* 40(1):79-91. https://doi.org /10.1086/268269.

Freese, Jeremy, and J. Alex Kevern. 2013. "Types of Causes." In *Handbook of Causal Analysis for Social Research*, Handbooks of Sociology and Social Research, edited by S. L. Morgan, 27-41. Dordrecht: Springer Netherlands.

Fridman, Daniel. 2016. *Freedom from Work: Embracing Financial Self-Help in the United States and Argentina*. Stanford, CA: Stanford University Press.

Friedman, Sam, and Daniel Laurison. 2019. *The Class Ceiling: Why It Pays to Be Privileged*. 1st ed. Bristol, UK: Policy Press.

Fusch, Patricia I., and Lawrence R. Ness. 2015. "Are We There Yet? Data Saturation in Qualitative Research." 20(9). https://doi.org/10.46743/2160 -3715/2015.2281.

Gansen, Heidi M. 2017. "Reproducing (and Disrupting) Heteronormativity: Gendered Sexual Socialization in Preschool Classrooms." *Sociology of Education* 90(3):255–72. https://doi.org/10.1177/0038040717720981.

———. 2018. "Push-Ups Versus Clean-Up: Preschool Teachers' Gendered Beliefs, Expectations for Behavior, and Disciplinary Practices." *Sex Roles*, July 19. https://doi.org/10.1007/s11199-018-0944-2.

Garcia, Angela S. 2019. *Legal Passing*. 1st ed. Oakland: University of California Press.

Gauchat, Gordon. 2012. "Politicization of Science in the Public Sphere: A Study of Public Trust in the United States, 1974 to 2010." *American Sociological Review* 77(2):167–87. https://doi.org/10.1177/0003122412438225.

Geertz, Clifford. 1973. *The Interpretation of Cultures*. New York: Basic Books.

Gerring, John. 2017. "Qualitative Methods." *Annual Review of Political Science* 20:15–36.

Gerson, Kathleen. 1985. *Hard Choices: How Women Decide about Work, Career and Motherhood*. Berkeley: University of California Press.

Gerson, Kathleen, and Sarah Damaske. 2020. *The Science and Art of Interviewing*. 1st ed. New York: Oxford University Press.

Gewin, Virginia. 2016. "Data Sharing: An Open Mind on Open Data." *Nature* 529(7584):117–19. https://doi.org/10.1038/nj7584-117a.

Gibson, Priscilla, and Laura Abrams. 2003. "Racial Difference in Engaging, Recruiting, and Interviewing African American Women in Qualitative Research." *Qualitative Social Work* 2(4):457–76. https://doi.org/10.1177 /1473325003024005.

Gillespie, Andra. 2013. *The New Black Politician: Cory Booker, Newark, and Post-Racial America*. New York: New York University Press.

Glaser, Barney, and Anselm Strauss. 1999. *The Discovery of Grounded Theory: Strategies for Qualitative Research*. New Brunswick, NJ: Routledge.

Gluck, Sherna Berger, and Daphne Patai. 1991. *Women's Words: The Feminist Practice of Oral History*. New York: Routledge.

Goffman, Erving. 1956. *Interaction Ritual: Essays in Face-to-Face Behavior.* New York: Routledge.

———. 1959. *The Presentation of Self in Everyday Life.* 1st ed. New York: Anchor.

Goldrick-Rab, Sara. 2016. *Paying the Price: College Costs, Financial Aid, and the Betrayal of the American Dream.* Chicago: University of Chicago Press.

Gonzales, Roberto G. 2011. "Learning to Be Illegal: Undocumented Youth and Shifting Legal Contexts in the Transition to Adulthood." *American Sociological Review* 76(4):602–19. https://doi.org/10.1177/0003122411411901.

Green, Judith, and Nicky Britten. 1998. "Qualitative Research and Evidence Based Medicine." *BMJ* 316(7139):1230–32. https://doi.org/10.1136/bmj.316 .7139.1230.

Greene, Melanie J. 2014. "On the Inside Looking In: Methodological Insights and Challenges in Conducting Qualitative Insider Research." *Qualitative Report* 19(29):1–13. https://doi.org/10.46743/2160-3715/2014.1106.

Guest, Greg, Arwen Bunce, and Laura Johnson. 2006. "How Many Interviews Are Enough? An Experiment with Data Saturation and Variability." *Field Methods* 18(1):59–82. https://doi.org/10.1177/1525822X05279903.

Guhin, Jeffrey. 2020. *Agents of God: Boundaries and Authority in Muslim and Christian Schools.* New York: Oxford University Press.

Güran, Gözde. 2020. "Brokers of Order: How Money Moves in Wartime Syria." PhD diss., Princeton University.

Hagerman, Margaret. 2018. *White Kids: Growing Up with Privilege in a Racially Divided America.* New York: New York University Press.

Hammersley, Martyn. 1992. "The Paradigm Wars: Reports from the Front." *British Journal of Sociology of Education* 13(1):131–43. https://doi.org/10 .1080/0142569920130110.

———. 2000. "The Relevance of Qualitative Research." *Oxford Review of Education* 26(3–4):393–405. https://doi.org/10.1080/713688545.

Hammersley, Martyn, and Paul Atkinson. 1995. *Ethnography: Principles in Practice.* East Sussex, UK: Psychology Press.

Harris, Anna, Andrea Wojcik, and Rachel Vaden Allison. 2020. "How to Make an Omelette: A Sensory Experiment in Team Ethnography." *Qualitative Research* 20(5):632–48. https://doi.org/10.1177/1468794119890543.

Hatchett, Shirley, and Howard Schuman. 1975. "White Respondents and Race-of-Interviewer Effects." *Public Opinion Quarterly* 39(4):523–28.

Hausheer, Roger. 1996. "Three Major Originators of the Concept of Ver-stehen: Vico, Herder, Schleiermacher." *Royal Institute of Philosophy Supplements* 41:47–72. https://doi.org/10.1017/S1358246100006044.

Head, Megan L., Luke Holman, Rob Lanfear, Andrew T. Kahn, and Michael D. Jennions. 2015. "The Extent and Consequences of P-Hacking in Science." *PLOS Biology* 13(3):e1002106. https://doi.org/10.1371/journal.pbio.1002106.

Heisenberg, W. 1977. "Remarks on the Origin of the Relations of Un-certainty." In *The Uncertainty Principle and Foundations of Quantum Mechanics, a Fifty Years Survey*, edited by W. Price and S. Chissick, 3–6. London: Wiley.

Hennink, Monique M., Bonnie N. Kaiser, and Vincent C. Marconi. 2017. "Code Saturation Versus Meaning Saturation: How Many Interviews Are Enough?" *Qualitative Health Research* 27(4):591–608. https://doi.org/10.1177/1049732316665344.

Henrich, Joseph, Steven J. Heine, and Ara Norenzayan. 2010. "Most People Are Not WEIRD." *Nature* 466(7302):29. https://doi.org/10.1038/466029a.

Hirschman, Daniel, and Elizabeth Popp Berman. 2014. "Do Economists Make Policies? On the Political Effects of Economics1." *Socio-Economic Review* 12(4):779–811. https://doi.org/10.1093/ser/mwu017.

Ho, Karen. 2009. *Liquidated: An Ethnography of Wall Street*. Illustrated ed. Durham, NC: Duke University Press Books.

Hoang, Kimberly Kay. 2015. *Dealing in Desire: Asian Ascendancy, Western Decline, and the Hidden Currencies of Global Sex Work*. Oakland: University of California Press.

Hochschild, Arlie Russell. 1989. *The Second Shift: Working Families and the Revolution at Home*. New York: Penguin Books.

———. 2016. *Strangers in Their Own Land: Anger and Mourning on the American Right*. New York: The New Press.

Hodgson, Geoffrey M. 2001. *How Economics Forgot History: The Problem of Historical Specificity in Social Science*. New York: Routledge.

Hodkinson, Paul. 2005. "'Insider Research' in the Study of Youth Cultures." *Journal of Youth Studies* 8(2):131–49. https://doi.org/10.1080/13676260500149238.

Hollstein, Betina. 2011. "Qualitative Approaches." In *The SAGE Handbook of Social Network Analysis*, 404–16. Thousand Oaks, CA: Sage.

Hopf, Ted. 2007. "The Limits of Interpreting Evidence." In *Theory and Evidence in Comparative Politics and International Relations, New Visions in Security*, edited by R. N. Lebow and M. I. Lichbach, 55–84. New York: Palgrave Macmillan US.

Hughes, Cayce C. 2021. "'A House But Not a Home': How Surveillance in Subsidized Housing Exacerbates Poverty and Reinforces Marginalization." *Social Forces* 100(1):293–315. https://doi.org/10.1093/sf/soaa108.

Humphreys, Michael. 2005. "Getting Personal: Reflexivity and Autoethnographic Vignettes." *Qualitative Inquiry* 11(6):840–60.

Jack, Anthony Abraham. 2019. *The Privileged Poor: How Elite Colleges Are Failing Disadvantaged Students*. 1st ed. Cambridge, MA: Harvard University Press.

Jarzabkowski, Paula, Rebecca Bednarek, and Laure Cabantous. 2015. "Conducting Global Team-Based Ethnography: Methodological Challenges and Practical Methods." *Human Relations* 68(1):3–33. https://doi.org/10.1177/0018726714535449.

Jensen, Peter S., Henry K. Watanabe, and John E. Richters. 1999. "Who's up First? Testing for Order Effects in Structured Interviews Using a Counterbalanced Experimental Design." *Journal of Abnormal Child Psychology* 27(6):439–45. https://doi.org/10.1023/A:1021927909027.

Jerolmack, Colin, and Shamus Khan. 2014. "Talk Is Cheap: Ethnography and the Attitudinal Fallacy." *Sociological Methods & Research* 43(2):178–209. https://doi.org/10.1177/0049124114523396.

Jerolmack, Colin, and Alexandra K. Murphy. 2019. "The Ethical Dilemmas and Social Scientific Trade-Offs of Masking in Ethnography." *Sociological Methods & Research* 48(4):801–27. https://doi.org/10.1177/0049124117701483.

Johansson, Eva E., Gunilla Risberg, and Katarina Hamberg. 2003. "Is Qualitative Research Scientific, or Merely Relevant?" *Scandinavian Journal of Primary Health Care* 21(1):10–14. https://doi.org/10.1080/02813430310000492.

Jones, Nikki. 2018. *The Chosen Ones: Black Men and the Politics of Redemption*. 1st ed. Oakland: University of California Press.

Kajanus, Anni, Katherine McAuliffe, Felix Warneken, and Peter R. Blake. 2019. "Children's Fairness in Two Chinese Schools: A Combined Ethnographic and Experimental Study." *Journal of Experimental Child Psychology* 177:282–96. https://doi.org/10.1016/j.jecp.2018.08.012.

Kane, Emily W., and Laura J. Macaulay. 1993. "Interviewer Gender and Gender Attitudes." *Public Opinion Quarterly* 57(1):1–28. https://doi.org/10 .1086/269352.

Kanter, Rosabeth Moss. 1977. *Men and Women of the Corporation: New Edition.* New York: Basic Books.

Katz, Jack. 2015. "A Theory of Qualitative Methodology: The Social System of Analytic Fieldwork." *Méthod(e)s: African Review of Social Sciences Methodology* 1(1–2):131–46. https://doi.org/10.1080/23754745.2015.1017282.

———. 2019. "Hot Potato Criminology: Ethnographers and the Shame of Poor People's Crimes." *Annual Review of Criminology* 2:21–52.

Kerr, Norbert L. 1998. "HARKing: Hypothesizing after the Results Are Known." *Personality and Social Psychology Review* 2(3):196–217. https://doi .org/10.1207/s15327957pspr0203_4.

Khan, Amina. 2019. "Study Linking Police Violence and Black Infants' Health Is Retracted." *Los Angeles Times*, December 16.

Khan, Shamus. 2012. *Privilege: The Making of An Adolescent Elite.* Princeton, NJ: Princeton University Press.

King, Gary, Robert O. Keohane, and Sidney Verba. 1994. *Designing Social Inquiry.* Princeton, NJ: Princeton University Press.

Klinenberg, Eric. 2018. *Palaces for the People: How Social Infrastructure Can Help Fight Inequality, Polarization, and the Decline of Civic Life.* 1st ed. New York: Crown.

Knapik, Mirjam. 2006. "The Qualitative Research Interview: Participants' Responsive Participation in Knowledge Making." *International Journal of Qualitative Methods* 5(3):77–93. https://doi.org/10.1177/160940690 600500308.

Konnikova, Maria. 2015. "How a Gay-Marriage Study Went Wrong." *New Yorker*, May 22.

Kratochwil, Friedrich V. 2007. "Evidence, Inference, and Truth as Problems of Theory Building in the Social Sciences." In *Theory and Evidence in Comparative Politics and International Relations, New Visions in Security*, edited by R. N. Lebow and M. I. Lichbach, 25–54. New York: Palgrave Macmillan US.

Krause, Monika. 2014. *The Good Project.* Chicago: University of Chicago Press.

Krystalli, Roxani. 2018. "Negotiating Data Management with the National Science Foundation: Transparency and Ethics in Research Relationships." https://connect.apsanet.org/interpretation/wp-content/uploads/sites/60 /2015/10/Krystalli-NSF-Data-Sharing-Memo_ForPosting_March2019.pdf.

Kwon, Hyeyoung. 2014. "The Hidden Injury of Class in Korean-American Language Brokers' Lives." *Childhood* 21(1):56–71. https://doi.org/10.1177 /0907568213483597.

Labaree, Robert V. 2002. "The Risk of 'Going Observationalist': Negotiating the Hidden Dilemmas of Being an Insider Participant Observer." *Qualitative Research* 2(1):97–122. https://doi.org/10.1177/1468794102002001641.

Lacy, Karyn. 2007. *Blue-Chip Black: Race, Class, and Status in the New Black Middle Class*. Oakland: University of California Press.

Lamont, Michèle, and Patricia White. 2005. *Workshop Participants & Attendees*. Washington, DC: National Science Foundation.

Landsberger, Henry A. 1958. *Hawthorne Revisited: Management and the Worker, Its Critics, and Developments in Human Relations in Industry*. 1st ed. Ithaca, NY: Cornell University Press.

Lareau, Annette. 2000. *Home Advantage: Social Class and Parental Intervention in Elementary Education*. New York: Rowman & Littlefield.

———. 2011. *Unequal Childhoods*. Berkeley: University of California Press.

———. 2021. *Listening to People: A Practical Guide to Interviewing, Participant Observation, Data Analysis, and Writing It All Up*. Chicago: University of Chicago Press.

Lareau, Annette, and Kimberly Goyette. 2014. *Choosing Homes, Choosing Schools*. New York: Russell Sage Foundation.

Lareau, Annette, and Jeffrey Shultz. 2019. *Journeys Through Ethnography: Realistic Accounts of Fieldwork*. New York: Routledge.

Lee, Jennifer, and Min Zhou. 2015. *The Asian American Achievement Paradox*. Illustrated ed. New York: Russell Sage Foundation.

Levers, Merry-Jo D. 2013. "Philosophical Paradigms, Grounded Theory, and Perspectives on Emergence." *SAGE Open* 3(4):2158244013517243. https:// doi.org/10.1177/2158244013517243.

Lewis, Amanda E. 2003. *Race in the Schoolyard: Negotiating the Color Line in Classrooms and Communities*. New Brunswick, NJ: Rutgers University Press.

Lewis, Amanda E., and John B. Diamond. 2015. *Despite the Best Intentions: How Racial Inequality Thrives in Good Schools*. New York: Oxford University Press.

Lewis-McCoy, R. L'Heureux. 2014. *Inequality in the Promised Land: Race, Resources, and Suburban Schooling*. Palo Alto, CA: Stanford University Press.

Lichterman, Paul. 2017. "Interpretive Reflexivity in Ethnography." *Ethnography* 18(1):35–45. https://doi.org/10.1177/1466138115592418.

Liebow, Elliott. 1967. *Tally's Corner: A Study of Negro Streetcorner Men*. Lanham, MD: Rowman & Littlefield.

Linville, Patricia W., Gregory W. Fischer, and Peter Salovey. 1989. "Perceived Distributions of the Characteristics of In-Group and out-Group Members: Empirical Evidence and a Computer Simulation." *Journal of Personality and Social Psychology* 57(2):165–88. https://doi.org/10.1037/0022-3514.57.2.165.

Lizardo, Omar. 2021. "Habit and the Explanation of Action." *Journal for the Theory of Social Behaviour* 51(3): 391–411. https://doi.org/10.1111/jtsb.12273.

Lubet, Steven. 2017. *Interrogating Ethnography: Why Evidence Matters*. Oxford: Oxford University Press.

MacLeod, Jay. 1987. *Ain't No Makin' It: Aspirations and Attainment in a Low-Income Neighborhood*. Boulder, CO: Routledge.

Maher, Thomas V., Charles Seguin, Yongjun Zhang, and Andrew P. Davis. 2020. "Social Scientists' Testimony before Congress in the United States between 1946–2016: Trends from a New Dataset." *PLOS ONE* 15(3):e0230104. https://doi.org/10.1371/journal.pone.0230104.

Mahoney, James. 2000. "Strategies of Causal Inference in Small-N Analysis." *Sociological Methods & Research* 28(4):387–424. https://doi.org/10.1177/0049124100028004001.

———. 2007. "Qualitative Methodology and Comparative Politics." *Comparative Political Studies* 40(2):122–44. https://doi.org/10.1177/0010414006296345.

Mannheimer, Sara, Amy Pienta, Dessislava Kirilova, Colin Elman, and Amber Wutich. 2019. "Qualitative Data Sharing: Data Repositories and Academic Libraries as Key Partners in Addressing Challenges." *American Behavioral Scientist* 63(5):643–64. https://doi.org/10.1177/0002764218784991.

Marcus, Adam. 2020. "'I'm Starting the Year off with Something I Didn't Expect to Ever Do: I'm Retracting a Paper.'" *Retraction Watch*. January 20. https://retractionwatch.com/2020/01/20/im-starting-the-year-off -with-something-i-didnt-expect-to-ever-do-im-retracting-a-paper/.

Marx, David M., and Phillip Atiba Goff. 2005. "Clearing the Air: The Effect of Experimenter Race on Target's Test Performance and Subjective Experience." *British Journal of Social Psychology* 44(4):645–57. https://doi.org/10 .1348/014466604X17948.

Marx, David M., and Jasmin S. Roman. 2002. "Female Role Models: Protecting Women's Math Test Performance." *Personality and Social Psychology Bulletin* 28(9):1183–93. https://doi.org/10.1177/01461672022812004.

Matthews, Morgan C. 2022. "Organizational Roots of Gender Polarization in the State Legislature." *Sociological Inquiry* 92(1): 244–69. https://doi.org /10.1111/soin.12447.

Mauthner, Natasha S., and Andrea Doucet. 2008. "'Knowledge Once Divided Can Be Hard to Put Together Again': An Epistemological Critique of Collaborative and Team-Based Research Practices." *Sociology* 42(5):971–85. https://doi.org/10.1177/0038038508094574.

Maxwell, Joseph A. 2013. *Qualitative Research Design: An Interactive Approach.* 3rd ed. Thousand Oaks, CA: Sage.

May, Reuben A. Buford, and Mary Pattillo-McCoy. 2000. "Do You See What I See? Examining a Collaborative Ethnography." *Qualitative Inquiry* 6(1):65–87. https://doi.org/10.1177/107780040000600105.

Mazelis, Joan Maya. 2016. *Surviving Poverty.* New York: New York University Press.

McFarland, Sam G. 1981. "Effects of Question Order on Survey Responses." *Public Opinion Quarterly* 45(2):208–15. https://doi.org/10.1086/268651.

McKenna, Elizabeth. 2019. "The Revolution Will Be Organized: Power and Protest in Brazil's New Republic, 1988–2018." PhD diss., University of California, Berkeley.

Mckenzie, Sean, and Cecilia Menjívar. 2011. "The Meanings of Migration, Remittances and Gifts: Views of Honduran Women Who Stay." *Global Networks* 11(1):63–81. https://doi.org/https://doi.org/10.1111/j.1471-0374 .2011.00307.x.

McKeown, Timothy J. 1999. "Case Studies and the Statistical Worldview." Review of *Designing Social Inquiry: Scientific Inference in Qualitative*

Research, edited by G. King, R. O. Keohane, and S. Verba. *International Organization* 53(1):161–90.

McLeod, Julie, and Kate O'Connor. 2021. "Ethics, Archives and Data Sharing in Qualitative Research." *Educational Philosophy and Theory* 53(5):523–35. https://doi.org/10.1080/00131857.2020.1805310.

Mead, George Herbert. 1934. *Mind, Self, and Society.* Chicago: University of Chicago Press.

Mears, Ashley. 2020. *Very Important People: Status and Beauty in the Global Party Circuit.* Princeton, NJ: Princeton University Press.

Menjívar, Cecilia. 2011. *Enduring Violence: Ladina Women's Lives in Guatemala.* Berkeley: University of California Press.

Merton, Robert K. 1972. "Insiders and Outsiders: A Chapter in the Sociology of Knowledge." *American Journal of Sociology* 78(1):9–47. https://doi.org /10.1086/225294.

———. 1973. *The Sociology of Science: Theoretical and Empirical Investigations.* Chicago: University of Chicago Press.

Messick, David M., and Diane M. Mackie. 1989. "Intergroup Relations." *Annual Review of Psychology* 40:45–81. https://doi.org/10.1146/annurev.ps .40.020189.000401.

Miles, Matthew B. 1979. "Qualitative Data as an Attractive Nuisance: The Problem of Analysis." *Administrative Science Quarterly* 24(4):590–601. https://doi.org/10.2307/2392365.

Miles, Matthew B., and A. Michael Huberman. 1994. *Qualitative Data Analysis: An Expanded Sourcebook.* Thousand Oaks, CA: Sage.

Miller-Idriss, Cynthia. 2018. *The Extreme Gone Mainstream: Commercialization and Far Right Youth Culture in Germany.* Princeton, NJ: Princeton University Press.

———. 2019. "Testimony of Dr. Cynthia Miller-Idriss." House Committee on Homeland Security. September 18. https://homeland.house.gov/imo /media/doc/Miller-Testimony.pdf.

Mills, C. Wright. 1940. "Situated Actions and Vocabularies of Motive." *American Sociological Review* 5(6):904–13. https://doi.org/10.2307/2084524.

Monahan, Torin, and Jill A. Fisher. 2010. "Benefits of 'Observer Effects': Lessons from the Field." *Qualitative Research* 10(3):357–76. https://doi.org /10.1177/1468794110362874.

Moore, David W. 2002. "Measuring New Types of Question-Order Effects: Additive and Subtractive." *Public Opinion Quarterly* 66(1):80–91.

Morris, Edward W. 2005. "From 'Middle Class' to 'Trailer Trash': Teachers' Perceptions of White Students in a Predominately Minority School." *Sociology of Education* 78(2):99–121. https://doi.org/10.1177/00380407 0507800201.

Morris, Monique. 2018. *Pushout: The Criminalization of Black Girls in Schools.* New York: The New Press.

Moses, Jonathon Wayne, and Torbjorn L. Knutsen. 2019. *Ways of Knowing: Competing Methodologies in Social and Political Research.* New York: Macmillan International Higher Education.

Moskos, Peter. 2009. *Cop in the Hood.* Princeton, NJ: Princeton University Press.

Mueller, Anna S., and Seth Abrutyn. 2016. "Adolescents under Pressure: A New Durkheimian Framework for Understanding Adolescent Suicide in a Cohesive Community." *American Sociological Review* 81(5):877–99. https://doi.org/10.1177/0003122416663464.

Murphy, Hannah, Lauren Keahey, Emma Bennett, Archie Drake, Samantha K. Brooks, and G. James Rubin. 2020. "Millennial Attitudes towards Sharing Mobile Phone Location Data with Health Agencies: A Qualitative Study." *Information, Communication & Society* 0(0):1–14. https://doi.org/10.1080 /1369118X.2020.1753798.

Murray, Brittany, Thurston Domina, Linda Renzulli, and Rebecca Boylan. 2019. "Civil Society Goes to School: Parent-Teacher Associations and the Equality of Educational Opportunity." *RSF: The Russell Sage Foundation Journal of the Social Sciences* 5(3):41–63. https://doi.org/10.7758/RSF.2019 .5.3.03.

Nastasi, Bonnie K., and Stephen L. Schensul. 2005. "Contributions of Qualitative Research to the Validity of Intervention Research." *Journal of School Psychology* 43(3):177–95. https://doi.org/ 10.1016/j.jsp.2005.04.003.

Nayak, Anoop. 2006. "After Race: Ethnography, Race and Post-Race Theory." *Ethnic and Racial Studies* 29(3):411–30. https://doi.org/10.1080/014198 70600597818.

Newman, Katherine S., and Rebekah Peeples Massengill. 2006. "The Texture of Hardship: Qualitative Sociology of Poverty, 1995–2005." *Annual Review*

of Sociology 32(1):423–46. https://doi.org/10.1146/annurev.soc.32.061604
.123122.

Nosek, Brian A., and D. Stephen Lindsay. 2018. "Preregistration Becoming
the Norm in Psychological Science." *APS Observer* 31(3). www.psychological
science.org/observer/preregistration-becoming-the-norm-in-psychological
-science.

Oeur, Freeden Blume. 2018. *Black Boys Apart: Racial Uplift and Respectability
in All-Male Public Schools.* Minneapolis: University of Minnesota Press.

Pacheco-Vega, Raul. 2020. "Using Ethnography in Comparative Policy
Analysis: Premises, Promises and Perils." In *Handbook of Research Methods
and Applications in Comparative Policy Analysis,* 312–22. Cheltenham, UK:
Elgar.

Paradis, Elise, and Gary Sutkin. 2017. "Beyond a Good Story: From Hawthorne Effect to Reactivity in Health Professions Education Research."
Medical Education 51(1):31–39. https://doi.org/10.1111/medu.13122.

Park, Bernadette, Charles M. Judd, and Carey S. Ryan. 1991. "Social Categorization and the Representation of Variability Information." *European
Review of Social Psychology* 2(1):211–45. https://doi.org/10.1080/14792779
143000079.

Pascoe, C. J. 2011. *Dude, You're a Fag: Masculinity and Sexuality in High School.*
2nd ed. Berkeley: University of California Press.

Pattillo, Mary. 1999. *Black Picket Fences: Privilege and Peril among the Black
Middle Class.* Chicago: University of Chicago Press.

Peabody, Robert L., Susan Webb Hammond, Jean Torcom, Lynne P. Brown,
Carolyn Thompson, and Robin Kolodny. 1990. "Interviewing Political
Elites." *PS: Political Science & Politics* 23(3):451–55. https://doi.org/10.2307
/419807.

Perry, H. W., Jr. 1994. *Deciding to Decide: Agenda Setting in the United States
Supreme Court.* 1st ed. Cambridge, MA: Harvard University Press.

Pezalla, Anne E., Jonathan Pettigrew, and Michelle Miller-Day. 2012.
"Researching the Researcher-as-Instrument: An Exercise in Interviewer
Self-Reflexivity." *Qualitative Research* 12(2):165–85. https://doi.org/10.1177
/1468794111422107.

Posey-Maddox, Linn. 2014. *When Middle-Class Parents Choose Urban Schools:
Class, Race, and the Challenge of Equity in Public Education.* Chicago:
University of Chicago Press.

Pugh, Allison J. 2013. "What Good Are Interviews for Thinking about Culture? Demystifying Interpretive Analysis." *American Journal of Cultural Sociology* 1(1):42–68. https://doi.org/10.1057/ajcs.2012.4.

Pustejovsky, James E., and James P. Spillane. 2009. "Question-Order Effects in Social Network Name Generators." *Social Networks* 31(4):221–29. https://doi.org/10.1016/j.socnet.2009.06.001.

Putnam, Robert D. 2001. *Bowling Alone: The Collapse and Revival of American Community*. New York: Simon & Schuster.

Quattrone, George A., and Edward E. Jones. 1980. "The Perception of Variability within In-Groups and Out-Groups: Implications for the Law of Small Numbers." *Journal of Personality and Social Psychology* 38(1):141–52. https://doi.org/10.1037/0022-3514.38.1.141.

Rafalow, Matthew H. 2020. *Digital Divisions: How Schools Create Inequality in the Tech Era*. 1st ed. Chicago: University of Chicago Press.

Ragin, Charles C., Joane Nagel, and Patricia White. 2004. *Workshop on Scientific Foundations of Qualitative Research*. Washington, DC: National Science Foundation.

Raudenbush, Danielle. 2020. *Health Care Off the Books*. Oakland: University of California Press.

Ray, Ranita. 2017. *The Making of a Teenage Service Class: Poverty and Mobility in an American City*. Oakland: University of California Press.

Reese, Stephen D., Wayne A. Danielson, Pamela J. Shoemaker, Tsan-Kuo Chang, and Huei-Ling Hsu. 1986. "Ethnicity-of-Interviewer Effects Among Mexican-Americans and Anglos." *Public Opinion Quarterly* 50(4):563–72. https://doi.org/10.1086/269004.

Reggev, Niv, Kirstan Brodie, Mina Cikara, and Jason Mitchell. 2019. "Human Face-Selective Cortex Does Not Distinguish between Members of a Racial Outgroup." *eNeuro* 7(3). https://doi.org/10.1523/ENEURO.0431-19.2020.

Resnick, Brian. 2018. "Social Science Replication Crisis: Studies in Top Journals Keep Failing to Replicate." *Vox*, 27 August. www.vox.com/science-and-health/2018/8/27/17761466/psychology-replication-crisis-nature-social-science.

———. 2021. "Psychology Is in a Replication Crisis. The Psychological Science Accelerator Is Trying to Fix It." *Vox*, August 7. www.vox.com/science-and-health/22360363/replication-crisis-psychological-science-accelerator.

Resnik, David B. 2011. "Scientific Research and the Public Trust." *Science and Engineering Ethics* 17(3):399–409. https://doi.org/10.1007/s11948-010 -9210-x.

Reyes, Victoria. 2018. "Three Models of Transparency in Ethnographic Research: Naming Places, Naming People, and Sharing Data." *Ethnography* 19(2):204–26. https://doi.org/10.1177/1466138117733754.

Riehl, Carolyn. 2001. "Bridges to the Future: The Contributions of Qualitative Research to the Sociology of Education." *Sociology of Education* 74:115–34. https://doi.org/10.2307/2673257.

Riessman, Catherine Kohler. 1987. "When Gender Is Not Enough: Women Interviewing Women." *Gender & Society* 1(2):172–207. https://doi.org/10 .1177/089124328700102004.

———. 1990. "Strategic Uses of Narrative in the Presentation of Self and Illness: A Research Note." *Social Science & Medicine* 30(11):1195–1200. https://doi.org/10.1016/0277-9536(90)90259-U.

Rinaldo, Rachel, and Jeffrey Guhin. 2019. "How and Why Interviews Work: Ethnographic Interviews and Meso-Level Public Culture." *Sociological Methods & Research* 0049124119882471. https://doi.org/10.1177/004912 4119882471.

Rios, Victor M. 2011. *Punished: Policing the Lives of Black and Latino Boys.* New York: New York University Press.

———. 2015. Review of *On the Run: Fugitive Life in an American City,* by Alice Goffman. *American Journal of Sociology* 121(1):306–8. https://doi.org/10 .1086/681075.

Rivera, Lauren A. 2016. *Pedigree: How Elite Students Get Elite Jobs.* Reprint ed. Princeton, NJ: Princeton University Press.

Romero, Mary. 2006. "Racial Profiling and Immigration Law Enforcement: Rounding Up of Usual Suspects in the Latino Community." *Critical Sociology* 32(2–3):447–73. https://doi.org/10.1163/156916306777835376.

Rubin, Mark. 2017. "When Does HARKing Hurt? Identifying When Different Types of Undisclosed Post Hoc Hypothesizing Harm Scientific Progress." *Review of General Psychology* 21(4):308–20. https://doi.org/10.1037 /gpr0000128.

Sadovnik, Alan R. 2006. "Qualitative Research and Public Policy." In *Handbook of Public Policy Analysis: Theory, Politics, and Methods,* edited by F. Fischer and G. J. Miller. Boca Raton, FL: CRC Press.

Saiedi, Nader. 1992. *The Birth of Social Theory*. Lanham, MD: University Press of America.

Schwartz, Martin D. 2000. "Methodological Issues in the Use of Survey Data for Measuring and Characterizing Violence Against Women." *Violence Against Women* 6(8):815–38. https://doi.org/10.1177/10778010022182164.

Scott, Marvin B., and Stanford M. Lyman. 1968. "Accounts." *American Sociological Review* 33(1):46–62. https://doi.org/10.2307/2092239.

Shaw, Clifford Robe. 1930. *The Natural History of a Delinquent Career*. New York: Praeger.

Shedd, Carla. 2015. *Unequal City: Race, Schools, and Perceptions of Injustice*. 1s ed. New York: Russell Sage Foundation.

Shuval, Kerem, Karen Harker, Bahman Roudsari, Nora E. Groce, Britain Mills, Zoveen Siddiqi, and Aviv Shachak. 2011. "Is Qualitative Research Second Class Science? A Quantitative Longitudinal Examination of Qualitative Research in Medical Journals." *PLOS ONE* 6(2):e16937. https://doi.org/10.1371/journal.pone.0016937.

Silva, Jennifer M. 2013. *Coming Up Short: Working-Class Adulthood in an Age of Uncertainty*. 1st ed. New York: Oxford University Press.

Simi, Pete, Kathleen Blee, Matthew DeMichele, and Steven Windisch. 2017. "Addicted to Hate: Identity Residual among Former White Supremacists." *American Sociological Review* 82(6):1167–87. https://doi.org/10.1177/0003122417728719.

Simmel, Georg. 1909. "The Problem of Sociology." *American Journal of Sociology* 15(3):289–320.

Simmons, Erica S., and Nicholas Rush Smith. 2019. "The Case for Comparative Ethnography." *Comparative Politics* 51(3):341–59. https://doi.org/10.5129/001041519X15647434969920.

Simmons, Joseph P., Leif D. Nelson, and Uri Simonsohn. 2011. "False-Positive Psychology: Undisclosed Flexibility in Data Collection and Analysis Allows Presenting Anything as Significant." *Psychological Science* 22(11):1359–66. https://doi.org/10.1177/0956797611417632.

Simon, Bernd, and Thomas F. Pettigrew. 1990. "Social Identity and Perceived Group Homogeneity: Evidence for the Ingroup Homogeneity Effect." *European Journal of Social Psychology* 20(4):269–86. https://doi.org/10.1002/ejsp.2420200402.

Sixsmith, Judith, Margaret Boneham, and John E. Goldring. 2003. "Accessing the Community: Gaining Insider Perspectives from the Outside." *Qualitative Health Research* 13(4):578–89. https://doi.org/10.1177/1049732302 250759.

Small, Mario Luis. 2004. *Villa Victoria*. Chicago: University of Chicago Press.

———. 2009a. "'How Many Cases Do I Need?': On Science and the Logic of Case Selection in Field-Based Research." *Ethnography* 10(1):5–38. https://doi.org/10.1177/1466138108099586.

———. 2009b. *Unanticipated Gains: Origins of Network Inequality in Everyday Life*. New York: Oxford University Press.

———. 2011. "How to Conduct a Mixed Methods Study: Recent Trends in a Rapidly Growing Literature." *Annual Review of Sociology* 37(1):57–86. https://doi.org/10.1146/annurev.soc.012809.102657.

———. 2015. "De-Exoticizing Ghetto Poverty: On the Ethics of Representation in Urban Ethnography." *City & Community* 14(4):352–58. https://doi.org/10.1111/cico.12137.

———. 2017a. *Someone to Talk To*. New York: Oxford University Press.

———. 2017b. "Testimony of Mario L. Small, Grafstein Family Professor of Sociology at Harvard University, Session on 'What We Do Together: The State of Social Capital in America Today.'" US Senate, Joint Economic Committee, May 17, Washington, DC.

———. 2018. "Rhetoric and Evidence in a Polarized Society." Paper presented at the Coming to Terms with a Polarized Society Series, ISERP, Columbia University.

Small, Mario Luis, and Jenna M. Cook. 2021. "Using Interviews to Understand Why: Challenges and Strategies in the Study of Motivated Action." *Sociological Methods & Research* 0049124121995552. https://doi.org/10.1177/0049124121995552.

Small, Mario Luis, Robert A. Manduca, and William R. Johnston. 2018. "Ethnography, Neighborhood Effects, and the Rising Heterogeneity of Poor Neighborhoods across Cities." *City & Community* 17(3):565–89. https://doi.org/10.1111/cico.12316.

Smith, Adam. 1822. *The Theory of Moral Sentiments*. Jonesboro, TN: J. Richardson.

Song, Miri, and David Parker. 1995. "Commonality, Difference and the Dynamics of Disclosure in In-Depth Interviewing." *Sociology* 29(2):241–56. https://doi.org/10.1177/0038038595029002004.

Soss, Joe. 1999. "Lessons of Welfare: Policy Design, Political Learning, and Political Action." *American Political Science Review* 93(2):363–80. https://doi.org/10.2307/2585401.

Stack, Carol. 1974. *All Our Kin.* New York: Harper.

Stuart, Forrest. 2016. *Down, Out, and Under Arrest: Policing and Everyday Life in Skid Row.* Chicago: University of Chicago Press.

———. 2020. *Ballad of the Bullet.* Princeton, NJ: Princeton University Press.

Stuber, Jenny. 2021. *Aspen and the American Dream: How One Town Manages Inequality in the Era of Supergentrification.* 1st ed. Oakland: University of California Press.

Swidler, Ann. 2013. *Talk of Love: How Culture Matters.* Chicago: University of Chicago Press.

Takacs, Christopher George. 2020. "Becoming Interesting: Narrative Capital Development at Elite Colleges." *Qualitative Sociology* 43(2):255–70. https://doi.org/10.1007/s11133-020-09447-y.

Tavory, Iddo, and Stefan Timmermans. 2014. *Abductive Analysis: Theorizing Qualitative Research.* Chicago: University of Chicago Press.

Taylor, Jodie. 2011. "The Intimate Insider: Negotiating the Ethics of Friendship When Doing Insider Research." *Qualitative Research* 11(1):3–22. https://doi.org/10.1177/1468794110384447.

Thorne, Barrie. 1999. *Gender Play.* New Brunswick, NJ: Rutgers University Press.

Toscano, Alberto. 2008. "The Culture of Abstraction." *Theory, Culture & Society* 25(4):57–75. https://doi.org/10.1177/0263276408091983.

Trnka, Radek, and Radmila Lorencova. 2016. *Quantum Anthropology: Man, Cultures, and Groups in a Quantum Perspective.* Prague: Charles University Karolinum Press.

Tsai, Alexander C., Brandon A. Kohrt, Lynn T. Matthews, Theresa S. Betancourt, Jooyoung K. Lee, Andrew V. Papachristos, Sheri D. Weiser, and Shari L. Dworkin. 2016. "Promises and Pitfalls of Data Sharing in Qualitative Research." *Social Science & Medicine* (1982) 169:191–98. https://doi.org/10.1016/j.socscimed.2016.08.004.

Twine, France Winddance. 2006. "Visual Ethnography and Racial Theory: Family Photographs as Archives of Interracial Intimacies." *Ethnic and Racial Studies* 29(3):487–511. https://doi.org/10.1080/01419870600597909.

Tyson, Karolyn. 2011. *Integration Interrupted: Tracking, Black Students, and Acting White after Brown*. New York: Oxford University Press.

US Conference of Catholic Bishops. 2021. "Twenty-First Sunday in Ordinary Time." *Daily Readings*. August 22. https://bible.usccb.org/bible/readings/082221.cfm.

Vaisey, Stephen. 2009. "Motivation and Justification: A Dual-Process Model of Culture in Action." *American Journal of Sociology* 114(6):1675–1715. https://doi.org/10.1086/597179.

Van Bavel, Jay J., Dominic J. Packer, and William A. Cunningham. 2008. "The Neural Substrates of In-Group Bias: A Functional Magnetic Resonance Imaging Investigation." *Psychological Science* 19(11):1131–39. https://doi.org/10.1111/j.1467-9280.2008.02214.x.

Van Cleve, Nicole Gonzalez. 2016. *Crook County: Racism and Injustice in America's Largest Criminal Court*. Stanford, CA: Stanford University Press.

Vargas, Robert. 2016. *Wounded City: Violent Turf Wars in a Chicago Barrio*. 1st ed. New York: Oxford University Press.

Vatican. 1993. *Catechism of the Catholic Church—Paragraph # 2357*. Vatican Library.

Vaughan, Diane. 2004. "Theorizing Disaster: Analogy, Historical Ethnography, and the Challenger Accident." *Ethnography* 5(3):315–47. https://doi.org/10.1177/1466138104045659.

Venkatesh, Sudhir Alladi. 2009. *Off the Books: The Underground Economy of the Urban Poor*. Cambridge, MA: Harvard University Press.

———. 2013. "The Reflexive Turn: The Rise of First-Person Ethnography." *The Sociological Quarterly* 54(1):3–8. https://doi.org/10.1111/tsq.12004.

Visweswaran, Kamala. 1997. "Histories of Feminist Ethnography." *Annual Review of Anthropology* 26:591–621.

Vitale, Dean C., Achilles A. Armenakis, and Hubert S. Feild. 2008. "Integrating Qualitative and Quantitative Methods for Organizational Diagnosis: Possible Priming Effects?" *Journal of Mixed Methods Research* 2(1):87–105. https://doi.org/10.1177/1558689807309968.

Watkins-Hayes, Celeste. 2019. *Remaking a Life: How Women Living with HIV/AIDS Confront Inequality*. Oakland: University of California Press.

Weber, Max. 1978. *Economy and Society: A New Translation*. Berkeley: University of California Press.

Wedeen, Lisa. 2010. "Reflections on Ethnographic Work in Political Science." *Annual Review of Political Science* 13:255–72.

Weiss, Robert S. 1995. *Learning from Strangers: The Art and Method of Qualitative Interview Studies*. New York: Simon and Schuster.

Weller, Susan C., Ben Vickers, H. Russell Bernard, Alyssa M. Blackburn, Stephen Borgatti, Clarence C. Gravlee, and Jeffrey C. Johnson. 2018. "Open-Ended Interview Questions and Saturation." *PLOS ONE* 13(6):e0198606. https://doi.org/10.1371/journal.pone.0198606.

West, Brady T., and Annelies G. Blom. 2017. "Explaining Interviewer Effects: A Research Synthesis." *Journal of Survey Statistics and Methodology* 5(2):175–211. https://doi.org/10.1093/jssam/smw024.

White, Ariel, Anton Strezhnev, Christopher Lucas, Dominika Kruszewska, and Connor Huff. 2018. "Investigator Characteristics and Respondent Behavior in Online Surveys." *Journal of Experimental Political Science* 5(1):56–67. https://doi.org/10.1017/XPS.2017.25.

White, Douglas, Douglas R. White, and Ulla Johansen. 2005. *Network Analysis and Ethnographic Problems: Process Models of a Turkish Nomad Clan*. Lanham, MD: Lexington Books.

Whitehead, Alfred North. 1925. *Science and the Modern World*. New York: Macmillan.

Whyte, William Foote. 1943. *Street Corner Society*. Chicago: University of Chicago Press.

Wicherts, Jelte M., Coosje L. S. Veldkamp, Hilde E. M. Augusteijn, Marjan Bakker, Robbie C. M. van Aert, and Marcel A. L. M. van Assen. 2016. "Degrees of Freedom in Planning, Running, Analyzing, and Reporting Psychological Studies: A Checklist to Avoid *p*-Hacking." *Frontiers in Psychology* 7. https://doi.org/10.3389/fpsyg.2016.01832.

Willis, Paul. 1977. *Learning to Labor: How Working-Class Kids Get Working-Class Jobs*. New York: Columbia University Press.

Wingfield, Adia Harvey. 2009. "Racializing the Glass Escalator: Reconsidering Men's Experiences with Women's Work." *Gender & Society* 23(1):5–26. https://doi.org/10.1177/0891243208323054.

Wingfield, Adia Harvey. 2010. "Are Some Emotions Marked 'Whites Only'? Racialized Feeling Rules in Professional Workplaces." *Social Problems* 57(2):251–68. https://doi.org/10.1525/sp.2010.57.2.251.

Wingfield, Adia Harvey, and Koji Chavez. 2020. "Getting in, Getting Hired, Getting Sideways Looks: Organizational Hierarchy and Perceptions of Racial Discrimination." *American Sociological Review* 85(1):31–57. https://doi.org/10.1177/0003122419894335.

Xu, Mengxuan Annie, and Gail Blair Storr. 2012. "Learning the Concept of Researcher as Instrument in Qualitative Research." *Qualitative Report* 17(42):1–18.https://doi.org/10.46743/2160-3715/2012.1768.

Zhou, Yuqing, Tianyu Gao, Ting Zhang, Wenxin Li, Taoyu Wu, Xiaochun Han, and Shihui Han. 2020. "Neural Dynamics of Racial Categorization Predicts Racial Bias in Face Recognition and Altruism." *Nature Human Behaviour* 4(1):69–87. https://doi.org/10.1038/s41562-019-0743-y.

Index

follow-up, in in-depth interviewing (*continued*)
(study of elite college students' use of narrative)

follow-up, in in-depth interviewing, specific example of (study of elite college students' use of narrative), 108–10

follow-up, in participant observation, two contexts of: in the field context, 110–14; outside the field context (seeking data outside the field site), 114–16. *See also* follow-up, in participant observation, specific example of (study of urban life among LBQ women)

follow-up, in participant observation, specific example of (study of urban life among LBQ women), 116–18

Geertz, Clifford, 27; on the concept of "thick description," 40

generalizability, 6, 8. *See also* representativeness

generalization from qualitative evidence, 61–64, 81–89; as it relates to heterogeneity, 61–64; as it relates to palpability, 81–89

Gina, interviews with, 85–86, 87–88, 89

Gone Home (Brown), 134–35

HARKing (writing up hypotheses after the results are known), 6

health care, study of access to, 75–78; access to health care as a "hybrid" of formal and informal elements, 78; lack of observable heterogeneity in, 77

heterogeneity, 9, 2178–79; background of, 48–50; depicting heterogeneity as characteristic of a group, 63; depicting heterogeneity as an exception to a group pattern, 61–62; depicting heterogeneity of experiences, 54–56, 72–73; depicting heterogeneity of motivation, 56; depicting heterogeneity of understanding, 53–54; high heterogeneity, 47; as an indicator of quality in data collection, 49; out-group heterogeneity bias, 48, 49; relation between empirical heterogeneity and theoretical concepts, 57–60, 61. *See also* diversity; heterogeneity, depicting the heterogeneity of experiences; heterogeneity, in in-depth interviewing; heterogeneity, in participant observation

heterogeneity, depicting the heterogeneity of experiences, 54–56, 72–73; depicting heterogeneity in a given experience, 71; at the group/collective level, 73–74; and an ethnographer's interest in a place rather than a person or set of persons, 74

heterogeneity, in in-depth interviewing, 50–51; and the individual, 51–53. *See also* heterogeneity, in in-depth interviewing, specific example of (study of low-income African American mothers living in subsidized housing in Houston)

National Science Foundation (NSF): and the increased number of submissions for qualitative research projects, 3; recommendations of to clarify the standards for rigorous qualitative research (including the minority report concerning), 3-4
Natural History of a Delinquent Career, The (Shaw), 52

observation, 22, 43, 51, 69, 73, 78, 81, 102, 143, 156, 157, 160, 173n17; ethnographic observation, 12, 18, 97, 109; observation protocols, 159. *See also* observer effect; participant observation; cognitive empathy, in participant observation; follow-up, in participant observation; homogeneity, in participant observation; palpability, in participant observation; self-awareness, in participant observation
observer effect, 120-21; "Hawthorne effect" version of, 120; "Heisenberg effect" version of, 120
Olivia, 68
out-groups, 48; out-group homogeneity bias, 48, 49

palpability, 21, 80, 99; example of effectively palpable reporting (how girls and boys play based on ethnographic observation), 97-98; improving the palpability of evidence, 92; palpability is not transparency, 171-72n4. *See also*

palpability, background of; palpability, in in-depth interviewing; palpability, in participant observation
palpability, background of: concreteness, 80-82; palpable statements/evidence, 82-84
palpability, in in-depth interviewing, 84-86; planned interviews, 86-88; unplanned interviews, 88-89; use of the deductive method in, 87-88. *See also* palpability, in in-depth interviewing, specific example of (study of children of immigrants)
palpability, in in-depth interviewing, specific example of (study of children of immigrants), 90-91
palpability, in participant observation, 91-92; and reporting of events, 92-95; and reporting on people, 95-96. *See also* palpability, in participant observation, specific example of (study of gender in children's play)
palpability, in participant observation, specific example of (study of gender in children's play), 97-98
participant observation, 17, 147, 151, 157; importance of involving all the senses in, 39; and the issue of narrative, 141-42; participant observation involves harm, 141; participant observers may differ in what they look for, 75; uncovering and inferring meaning in, 41-42. *See also* observation; cognitive empathy, in participant

observation; follow-up, in participant observation; heterogeneity, in participant observation; palpability, in participant observation; self-awareness, in participant observation
Pattillo-McCoy, Mary, 52, 100
p-hacking (mishandling data to produce significant findings), 6
political science, 5
political scientists, 2
proposals for research, evaluation of, 145–51
psychology, 5, 164n4, 166n32, 173n17
public opinion, 1

qualitative proposals, notes concerning, 155; anticipated follow-up concerning, 160–61; difficulty of evaluating proposals, 155–57; and exposure, 157–58; and preliminary data, 58; rationale concerning, 158–59; and self-awareness, 159–60
qualitative research, 10, 164n3; diversity of, 145–46; empirical qualitative research, 23, 24, 58, 115, 148, 155; as essential to a cumulative social science, 147; evaluation of, 22, 148–51; as an iterative process, 157; qualitative field studies, 168n58; transparency of, 7; three different elements that "qualitative" research refers to (type of data, method of data collection, data analysis), 9; use of the deductive method in, 58–59; use of the inductive method in,

59–60; what is "qualitative research," 8–9
qualitative researchers, in sociology, 6–7, 28, 146, 156, 157, 170n8, 175–76n5; importance to scientists, policy makers, and the public regarding current issues, 2; and the "paradigm wars" with quantitative researchers, 1
qualitative social science, 166n32; disagreements on what constitutes good qualitative social science, 2–3; qualitative sociologists, 2
quality, assessment of, 3–5
quantitative researchers, in sociology: and the "paradigm wars" with qualitative researchers, 1; accusations made during the "paradigm wars"; 1; the upper hand of quantitative research during the "paradigm wars," 1–2
"question-order effects," 66. *See also* surveys

random sampling, 15–16, 151; as an unhelpful indicator of quality in qualitative research, 15–16, 20, 85, 150–51. *See also* representative samples
Raudenbush, Danielle, 75–78
reflexivity, 121, 141. *See also* self-awareness
Remaking a Life (Watkins-Hayes), 52
Ren, 93–94, 95
reliability, x, 3, 13–14,142; as it relates to research conducted by outsiders, 142; as it relates to public mistrust of science, 6

reporting percentages from in-depth interviews, promise and peril of, 63–67

representative samples, x, 15–16, 20, 150–151, 173n21; as an unhelpful indicator of quality in qualitative research, 15–16, 20, 85, 150–51; complementing interview research with surveys using 67, 105–106; complementing participant observations with 115. *See also* random sampling

representativeness, x, 20, 115, 150, 161. *See also* generalizability

research design, 17, 49–50, 155–56; conception of, 15–16

research habits, 6

research objectives, 15–16

research sites, revisiting of, 166n32

sample size, 15, 19–20, 151; as an unhelpful indicator of quality in qualitative research, 19–20, 157–158. *See also* exposure

"sampling bias," 15, 16

"saturation": saturation sampling method, 109; topic saturation, 107

"selection bias," 16

self-awareness, 21–22, 119, 144, 159–60; background of, 120–22; example of the value of self-awareness for effective access to a specific population, 142–43; high self-awareness, 119; in in-depth interviewing, 124–34; and a self-reflective researcher, 121–22; the importance of self-awareness in gaining access to a population

before interviews begin, 134–35. *See also* observer effect; self-awareness, contexts of; self-awareness, in in-depth interviews; self-awareness, in participant observation

self-awareness, contexts of: access, 122, 136–39; disclosure, 122–23, 139–40; interpretation, 123–24, 140–42

self-awareness, in in-depth interviewing, 124–35. *See also* self-awareness, in in-depth interviewing, specific example of (study of race relations and politics in Appalachia)

self-awareness, in in-depth interviewing, specific example of (study of race relations and politics in Appalachia), 134–35

self-awareness, in participant observations, 135–43. *See also* self-awareness, in participant observations, specific example of (study of family support networks in an African American urban neighborhood)

self-awareness, in participant observations, specific example of (study of family support networks in an African American urban neighborhood), 142–43

sexuality, LBGTQ and Catholic young adults' view of their church's teachings on (access domain of), 124–29; and the Catholic Church's official view of homosexuality, 125–26, 130; participants in, 126;

Founded in 1893,
UNIVERSITY OF CALIFORNIA PRESS
publishes bold, progressive books and journals
on topics in the arts, humanities, social sciences,
and natural sciences—with a focus on social
justice issues—that inspire thought and action
among readers worldwide.

The UC PRESS FOUNDATION
raises funds to uphold the press's vital role
as an independent, nonprofit publisher, and
receives philanthropic support from a wide
range of individuals and institutions—and from
committed readers like you. To learn more, visit
ucpress.edu/supportus.

Milton Keynes UK
Ingram Content Group UK Ltd.
UKHW041929140924
448311UK00003B/13

9 780520 390669